# EASY STEPS IN ENGLISH SPELLING

# STEP THREE

**WHEATON**

*A Member of the Pergamon Group*

This edition first published in 1968

Printed in Great Britain by A. Wheaton and Co. Ltd, Exeter

08 008732 9

# PREFACE

The three books of this series attempt to set out a rationalized scheme for the teaching of spelling and, at the same time, to make the subject as easy and interesting as possible. This third book is appropriate to the work of the Secondary School. Here again, the material is divided into two parts representing two distinct levels of difficulty. The parts are bound together for convenience in revision and to provide ample material for the most advanced pupils. No pupil, of course, is expected to master all the words in the book.

# HOW TO TEACH SPELLING

The average child does not find spelling difficult once he realizes the purpose of its study and his interest is thoroughly aroused.

The key to the correct spelling of words is **memorization by actual use in a suitable context.**

Method of Teaching:

1. Present all new words in a suitable context (either phrase or sentence) selected from the class reading matter or composition, training every child in the "dictionary habit".
2. Write these contexts up on the blackboard and have them read aloud. Write the new words in a different coloured chalk.
3. Have language lessons with selected words. Let the pupils construct a variety of sentences containing them, or provide sentences with blanks to be filled in with the appropriate words.
4. Give word-building exercises on such words as lend themselves to this method of treatment. This will include allied words or derivatives.
5. A little intensive drill in the form of repetition may be necessary for some children.
6. Keep a class word-book and let every pupil keep a word-book of his own.
7. Test by dictation.

# contents

# PART ONE

## 1. Simple Spelling Rules

*An* affix (= *something fixed to*) *consists of a letter or several letters forming one or more syllables that may be put before or after a word to change or modify its meaning. Affixes put in front of a word are called* prefixes, *and those put at the end of a word are called* suffixes.

<u>RULE 1</u>. Words ending in a single consonant and accented on the last syllable double the final consonant before an affix beginning with a vowel.

| | | | |
|---|---|---|---|
| admit | admitting | admitted | admittance |
| commit | committing | committed | (commitment)* |
| omit | omitting | omitted | |
| transmit | transmitting | transmitted | transmitter |
| deter | deterring | deterred | deterrence |
| bestir | bestirring | bestirred | |
| remit | remitting | remitted | remittance |
| submit | submitting | submitted | |
| allot | allotting | allotted | (allotment) |
| transfer | transferring | transferred | (transference) |
| refer | referring | referred | (reference) |
| occur | occurring | occurred | occurrence |
| regret | regretting | regretted | |

*Final consonant not doubled in words in brackets.

# <u>RULE</u> 2. Words ending in **l** also follow rule 1.

*Accented on the first syllable:*

| | | | |
|---|---|---|---|
| quarrel | quarrelling | quarrelled | (quarrelsome) |
| travel | travelling | travelled | traveller |
| cancel | cancelling | cancelled | cancellation |
| counsel | counselling | counselled | counsellor |
| chisel | chiselling | chiselled | chiseller |
| model | modelling | modelled | modeller |
| marshal | marshalling | marshalled | |
| gambol | gambolling | gambolled | |
| equal | equalling | equalled | (equality) |
| marvel | marvelling | marvelled | marvellous |
| shovel | shovelling | shovelled | shoveller |
| grovel | grovelling | grovelled | groveller |
| shrivel | shrivelling | shrivelled | |
| imperil | imperilling | imperilled | |
| rival | rivalling | rivalled | (rivalry) |
| revel | revelling | revelled | reveller |
| jewel | jewelling | jewelled | jeweller |
| victual | victualling | victualled | victualler |

*Accented on the last syllable:*

| | | | |
|---|---|---|---|
| excel | excelling | excelled | ex'cellent |
| extol | extolling | extolled | |
| expel | expelling | expelled | (explusion) |
| enrol | enrolling | enrolled | (enrolment) |
| patrol | patrolling | patrolled | |
| distil | distilling | distilled | distillery |
| propel | propelling | propelled | propeller |

*Accented on the middle syllable:*

| | | |
|---|---|---|
| apparel | apparelling | apparelled |
| dishevel | dishevelling | dishevelled |

RULE 3. Most nouns accented on the first syllable and ending in a single consonant do not double the final consonant.

| | | | |
|---|---|---|---|
| credit | crediting | credited | creditor |
| benefit | benefiting | benefited | |
| parallel | | paralleled | parallelogram |
| covet | coveting | coveted | covetous |
| gossip | gossiping | gossiped | gossipy |
| murmur | murmuring | murmured | murmurer |
| conquer | conquering | conquered | conqueror |
| pocket | pocketing | pocketed | |
| market | marketing | marketed | |
| suffer | suffering | suffered | sufferance |
| rivet | riveting | riveted | riveter |
| utter | uttering | uttered | utterance |
| profit | profiting | profited | profiteer |
| combat | combating | combated | |
| gallop | galloping | galloped | galloper |
| edit | editing | edited | editor |

*Note that final consonant is not doubled before* **-able, -ence**:

| | | |
|---|---|---|
| preferable | preference | conference |
| referable | reference | deference |
| transferable | transference | |

RULE 4. Most words ending in double consonants remain unchanged before a suffix.

| | | | |
|---|---|---|---|
| progress | progressing | progressed | progressive |
| suggest | suggesting | suggested | suggestive |
| exhaust | exhausting | exhausted | exhaustion |
| discern | discerning | discerned | discernible |
| design | designing | designed | designer |

8

**RULE 5.** Final **e** is dropped mostly before vowel suffixes.

| | | | |
|---|---|---|---|
| besieging | notable | perseverance | stony |
| balancing | procurable | resemblance | smoky |
| practising | desirable | contrivance | spongy |
| recognizing | excitable | civilization | virtuous |
| persevering | excusable | assemblage | bluish |
| pursuing | incurable | purchasable | roguish |
| torturing | advisable | conceivable | humanity |
| besieged | blamable | lovable | maturity |
| interfered | untamable | slavish | insanity |

*Final* **e** *dropped before some consonants:*

**duly, truly, wholly, awful, feebly, suitably, argument.**

**RULE 6.** Final **e** is retained mostly before consonantal suffixes.

| | | | |
|---|---|---|---|
| extremely | senseless | graceful | bereavement |
| decisively | tiresome | remorseless | hoarseness |
| supremely | defenceless | lonesome | sameness |
| immensely | revengeful | troublesome | wholesome |
| sincerely | shameful | elopement | atonement |
| submissively | remorseful | commencement | doleful |
| solely | peaceful | advertisement | tuneful |

*Final* **e** *retained also before some vowel suffixes, particularly after* **c** *and* **g**:

| | | | |
|---|---|---|---|
| peaceable | changeable | manageable | agreeing |
| traceable | marriageable | chargeable | shoeing |
| noticeable | courageous | saleable | agreeable |
| serviceable | vengeance | dyeing | disagreeable |

<u>RULE 7</u>. Final **ll** changes to **l** in certain combinations.

**skilful, wilful, distil, until, instil, enrol, fulfil, spiteful, welfare, welcome, belfry, bulrush.**

*But final **ll** unchanged in:*

**recall, illwill, unroll, befall, befell, bullfinch, downfall, smallness, millstone, farewell.**

<u>RULE 8</u>. Words ending in **y** preceded by a vowel retain **y** before a suffix.

| Nouns | | Noun plurals | |
|---|---|---|---|
| **employment** | **annoyance** | **moneys** | **attorneys** |
| **betrayal** | **enjoyment** | **turnkeys** | **viceroys** |
| **prayer** | **surveyor** | **envoys** | **essays** |

| Verbs | | | |
|---|---|---|---|
| **obeys** | **conveys** | **purvey** | **portray** |
| **obeying** | **conveying** | **purveying** | **portraying** |
| **obeyed** | **conveyed** | **purveyed** | **portrayed** |

<u>RULE 9</u>. Words ending in **y** preceded by a consonant change **y** into **i** except before **-ing.**

| Noun plurals | | Adjectives | |
|---|---|---|---|
| **burglaries** | **auxiliaries** | **injurious** | **industrious** |
| **anniversaries** | **ecstasies** | **studious** | **industrial** |
| **anxieties** | **gaities** | **magnificent** | **victorious** |
| **societies** | **prophecies** | **wearisome** | **enviable** |
| **diaries** | **lullabies** | **y** *changed to* **e** *instead of* **i** | |
| **abilities** | **energies** | | |
| **salaries** | **possibilities** | **bounteous** | **beauteous** |

|  | Nouns | | Verbs |
| --- | --- | --- | --- |
| cleanliness | hardihood | sympathize | satisfied |
| mutineer | librarian | prophesies | petrified |

Exceptions: **babyish, slyness.**

**y** *retained before* **-ing:**

| | | | |
| --- | --- | --- | --- |
| carrying | tarrying | magnifying | qualifying |
| studying | fortifying | prophesying | accompanying |

RULE 10. Use of prefixes **dis-** and **mis-**: two **s**s occur only when the root begins with an **s**. The root is that part of a word which conveys its essential meaning.

| One s | Two ss | One s | Two ss |
| --- | --- | --- | --- |
| disappoint | dissuade | misbehave | mis-spell |
| disloyal | dissolve | misadventure | mis-spelt |
| disapprove | dissolution | misbelieve | mis-spend |
| discourtesy | dissent | mistrust | mis-spent |
| disqualify | dissension | misuse | mis-shapen |
| disagreeable | dissect | misbehaviour | mis-speak |
| distribute | dissimilar | mistaken | mis-seeming |

RULE 11. Distinguish between words beginning with **de-** and with **dis-**. Correct enunciation is an aid to correct spelling.

| | | | |
| --- | --- | --- | --- |
| descent | describe | dissent | dissolve |
| descend | despond | disciple | disrupt |
| desert | despise | discern | display |
| despair | desire | distaste | disport |

# RULE 12. Use of **ie** or **ei**:

Key-word **lice**
after **l** comes **i**
after **c** comes **e**

| | | | | |
|---|---|---|---|---|
| retrieve | wield | seize | skein | believe |
| reprieve | fiendish | seizure | freight | relieve |
| frieze | mischievous | weir | sleight | conceive |
| siege | achieve | sheik | eider | conceit |
| besiege | achievement | weird | feint | deceive |
| grief | sieve | heinous | | deceit |
| grievous | | leisure | | receive |
| aggrieve | | | | receipt |

## 2. NOUN PLURALS

*Nouns used in plural only:*

**trousers, breeches, scissors, pincers, forceps, measles, politics, physics, mathematics, tidings.**

*Some rare plurals :*

| Singular | Plural | Singular | Plural |
|---|---|---|---|
| **cameo** | **cameos** | **stratum** | **strata** |
| **analysis** | **analyses** | **genus** | **genera** |
| **chrysalis** | **chrysalides** | **antenna** | **antennae** |
| **oasis** | **oases** | **memorandum** | **memoranda** |
| **axis** | **axes** | **phenomenon** | **phenomena** |
| **basis** | **bases** | **genie** | **genii** |
| **radius** | **radii** | **genius** | **geniuses** |
| **terminus** | **termini** | **cherub** | **cherubim** |

## 3. POSSESSIVE CASE OF NOUNS

*The following three simple rules cover every instance in which a noun has to be written in the possessive case:*

First write down the name of the possessor or possessors.

Then add an apostrophe (').

Lastly add **s** if it is sounded in speech, but not other-wise.

*Apply these rules to the following:*

| POSSESSIVE SINGULAR | POSSESSIVE PLURAL |
|---|---|
| **summer's** sun | **thieves'** slang |
| **sheep's** back | **sheep's** backs |
| **chief's** authority, | **ships'** anchors, |
| **master's** voice | **masters'** voices |
| **James's** collars | **birds'** parliament, |
| **fox's** cunning | **foxes'** den |
| **lady's** maids | **ladies'** maids |
| **deer's** enclosure | **deer's** enclosure |
| for **conscience'** sake | **farmers'** foes, |
| for **Jesus'** sake | **mice's** nest |
| **son-in-law's** brother | **sons-in-law's** brothers |
| **woman's** wiles | **women's** wiles |

## 4. DRILL IN VERB TENSES

| PRESENT TIME Today, I | PAST TIME Yesterday, I | INCOMPLETE ACTION I am, was, shall be | COMPLETED ACTION I have, I had |
|---|---|---|---|
| **lie** | **lay** | **lying** | **lain** |
| **lie** | **lied** | **lying** | **lied** |
| **lay** | **laid** | **laying** | **laid** |
| **lose** | **lost** | **losing** | **lost** |
| **weave** | **wove** | **weaving** | **woven** |
| **bid** | **bade** | **bidding** | **bidden** |
| **win** | **won** | **winning** | **won** |
| **awake** | **awoke** | **awaking** | **awoke** |
| **strew** | **strewed** | **strewing** | **strewn** |
| **mow** | **mowed** | **mowing** | **mown** |

13

| PRESENT TIME Today, I | PAST TIME Yesterday, I | INCOMPLETE ACTION I am, was, shall be | COMPLETED ACTION I have, I had |
|---|---|---|---|
| chide | chid | chiding | chidden |
| climb | climbed | climbing | climbed |
| cling | clung | clinging | clung |
| flee | fled | fleeing | fled |
| hang | hang / hanged | hanging | hung / hanged |
| heave | heaved (hove) | heaving | heaved |
| shake | shook | shaking | shaken |
| shear | sheared | shearing | shorn or sheared |
| slide | slid | sliding | slid |
| slink | slunk | slinking | slunk |
| smite | smote | smiting | smitten |
| speed | sped | speeding | sped |
| spring | sprang | springing | sprung |
| swim | swam | swimming | swum |
| tear | tore | tearing | torn |
| thrive | throve | thriving | thriven |

*Replace* **write** *by other verbs, as* **speak, lie,** *etc., in the following tenses:*

| | |
|---|---|
| I write | We write |
| You write | You write |
| He writes | They write |
| I am writing | We are writing |
| You are writing | You are writing |
| He is writing | They are writing |
| I wrote | We wrote |
| You wrote | You wrote |
| He wrote | They wrote |

| | |
|---|---|
| I was **writing** | We were **writing** |
| You were **writing** | You were **writing** |
| He was **writing** | They were **writing** |
| I have **written** | We have **written** |
| You have **written** | You have **written** |
| He has **written** | They have **written** |
| I had **written** | We had **written** |
| You had **written** | You had **written** |
| He had **written** | They had **written** |
| I shall **write** | We shall **write** |
| You will **write** | You will **write** |
| He will **write** | They will **write** |
| I shall have **written** | We shall have **written** |
| You will have **written** | You will have **written** |
| He will have **written** | They will have **written** |

## 5. CONSONANTAL SOUNDS

*Use a dictionary to find the meaning of:*

c = k      **elastic, vacuum, secretary, puncture, landscape, technical, cupidity, spectacle, crystal, academy, barnacles, buccaneer, massacre.**

c = s      **anticipate, science, ceiling, citadel, cereal, precipice, precipitous, cylinder, placid, pacify, menace, porcelain, legacy, incident, vicinity, reconcile, adjacent, cigar, cigarette, disciple, discipline.**

ch = k      **orchid, scheme, architect, melancholy, sepulchre, character, chaos, chasm.**

ch = sh      **chaise, chevalier.**

g = j      **tragedy, congeal, digest, cudgel, elegy, frigid, gipsy, pageant, menagerie, magistrate, exaggerate, legible, lounging.**

| ph = f | phrase, pamphlet, phosphorus, caliph, trophy, sphinx, cipher, diphthong, alphabet, phantom, physic, physician. |
|---|---|
| que = k | cheque, unique, picturesque. |
| qu = kw | sequel, aquatic, aquiline, quotient, equable, equity, equation, marquis. |
| s = z | president, diocese, museum, enthusiasm, venison. |

| tial<br>cial | = shal | essential, partial, substantial, commercial. |
|---|---|---|
| cious<br>tious<br>xious<br>scious | = shus | suspicious, luscious, audacious, ferocious, vicious, spacious, noxious, vexatious, conscious, unconscious. |

*Some double consonants :*

| | | | |
|---|---|---|---|
| abbreviate | woollen | innumerable | associate |
| accumulate | syllable | apparatus | battalion |
| college | collision | hippopotamus | accidental |
| moccasin | appalling | embarrass | succulent |
| occasion | miscellaneous | assailed | alluvial |
| occurrence | illuminate | stirred | Mississippi |
| parricide | tranquillity | assassin | committee |
| toboggan | compelled | harassing | attached |

# 6. SYLLABIFICATION AND ACCENTUATION

Words are composed of either one or more syllables. A syllable is a word or part of a word that is uttered by a single effort of the voice. In separating words into syllables, group together letters that are sounded together.

If you need to break a word when writing, always do so between two syllables.

| | | | |
|---|---|---|---|
| ad'-e-quate | vol'-un-ta-ry | sub'sti-tute | com'-po-site |
| il'-lus-trate | an'-al-yse | re'-qui-site | pref'-ace |
| ad'-mir-able | par'-ti-cle | ex'-qui-site | vul'-ner-a-ble |
| ex'-cel-lent | nec'-es-sa-ry | for'-mid-a-ble | im'-pe-tus |
| rep'-ri-mand | in'-ter-est | ad'-ver-sa-ry | or'-ches-tra |
| ap'-er-ture | cab'-i-net | es'-ti-ma-ble | sep'-ar-ate |
| bal'-lad | hom'-age | sig'-ni-fy | vig'-or-ous-ly |
| prot'-es-tant | pre'-fect | pref'-er-ence | per'-i-scope |
| talk'-a-tive | lig'-nite | fran'-chise | frag'-ile |
| dis'-ci-pline | rec'-i-pe | fu'-ri-ous-ly | u'-til-lize |
| mis'-chiev-ous | av'-a-lanche | cap'-it-al-ist | al'-ge-bra |
| me'-te-or | pa'-tri-arch | pa'-tr-iot | phos'-phor-us |
| mag'-net-ism | sap'-phire | diph'-thong | bach'-e-lor |
| fu'-mi-gate | den'-i-zen | arch'-i-tect | ex'-e-cute |

*Accent on second syllable:*

| | | | | |
|---|---|---|---|---|
| mo-les'-ted | in-ter'-pret | su-per'-flu-ous | ob-scu'-ri-ty | |
| in-quis'-i-tive | in-trep'-id | in-sep'-ar-a-ble | ho-ri'-zon | |
| in-ter'-ment | se-date'-ly | cer-tif'-i-cate | con-tin'-gent | |
| pro-lif'-ic | im-preg'-na-ble | al-lot'-ment | di-rec'-to-ry | |
| di-am'-e-ter | pho-tog'-ra-phy | al-ter'-na-tive | an-al'-y-sis | |
| sal-i'-va | o-a'-sis | col-lapse' | op-po'-nent | |
| his-tor'-i-cal | pa-vil'-i-on | dis-ci'-ple | so-ci'-e-ty | |
| di-vis'-i-ble | hy-e'-na | med-ic'-in-al | ad-ja'-cent | |
| a-dieu' | a-ward' | va-lise' | dis-sent' | in-trigue' |
| a-ghast' | rou-tine' | a-byss' | ga-zette' | ra-pine' |
| e-rase' | pre-cise' | tat-too' | u-nique' | di-seased' |
| cam-paign' | dis-cern' | a-wry' | im-merse' | ca-ress' |
| un-couth' | di-vulge' | o-blique' | o-paque' | di-vine' |

| | | | |
|---|---|---|---|
| sep-ar-a'-tion | pal-i-sade' | sci-en-tif'-ic | in-gen-u'-i-ty |
| en-gin-eer' | mar-guer-ite' | dis-tri-bu'-tion | |
| | | | in-qui-si'-tion |
| su-per-fi'-cial | rec-om-mend' | per-i-od'-ic | re-pe-ti'-tion |

*Meaning varying with accent:*

Use a dictionary to find the meaning of each word.

### (a) Noun and adjective

| | | | |
|---|---|---|---|
| ex'-pert | ex-pert' | in'-valid | in-val'-id |
| min'-ute | min-ute' | Au'-gust | au-gust' |

### (b) Noun and verb

| | | | |
|---|---|---|---|
| ac'-cent | ac-cent' | ex'-tract | ex-tract' |
| af'-fix | af-fix' | con'-tract | con-tract' |
| con'-cert | con-cert' | con'-test | con-test' |
| ob'-ject | ob-ject' | pro'-test | pro-test' |
| ex'-tract | ex-tract' | es'-cort | es-cort' |
| sub'-ject | sub-ject' | in'-crease | in-crease' |
| pro'-gress | pro-gress' | in'-cense | in-cense' |
| en'-vel-ope | en-vel'-op | ex'-ploit | ex-ploit' |
| des'-ert | de-sert' | ex'-port | ex-port' |
| con'-duct | con-duct' | im'-port | im-port' |
| con'-trast | con-trast' | con'-vict | con-vict' |
| sur'-vey | sur-vey' | prod-'uce | pro-duce' |
| per'-mit | per-mit' | at'-tribute | at-trib'-ute |

### (c) Adjective and verb

| | | | |
|---|---|---|---|
| ab'-sent | ab-sent' | fre'-quent | fre-quent' |

### (d) Noun or adjective and verb

| | | | |
|---|---|---|---|
| ab'-stract | ab-stract' | reb'-el | re-bel' |
| com'-pound | com-pound' | ref'-use | re-fuse' |
| se'-cret | se-crete' | pres'-ent | pre-sent' |

# 7. Pronounce And Spell

**ce, ci** *or* **ti** = she

**quotient** (kwo'-shent), the result of division.

**oceanic** (o-she-an'-ik), pertaining to the ocean.

**excruciate** (eks-kru'-she-ate), to inflict severe pain on.

**appreciate** (ap-pree'-she-ate), to value rightly.

**species** (spee'-sheeze), a classified group.

**glacial** (glay'-she-al), pertaining to ice, icy.

**associate** (a-so'-she-ate), to join or unite with.

**initiate** (in-i'-she-ate), to begin.

**negotiate** (nee-go'-she-ate), to arrange by discussion, to bargain.

**r** *to be sounded in:*

**easterly, westerly, northerly, southerly, February, library, secretary, gorse, arbitary.**

**remonstrate** (rem'-on-strate), to protest.

**demonstrate** (dem'-on-strate), to show.

# 8. Words To Be Distinguished

**accede,** to agree to.
**exceed,** to go beyond.

**accept,** to take.
**except,** to leave out, exclude.

**affect,** to influence.
**effect,** to produce; (n.) result.
**infect,** to taint, as with disease.
**defect,** something wanting, deficiency, fault.

**calendar,** a table of days and months.
**colander,** a utensil used for straining boiled vegetables.

**concert,** a musical entertainment.
**consort,** a partner, companion.

**corps** (pronounce *kor*), a division of an army (pl. **corps**, pronounce *korz*).
**corpse,** the dead body of a human being.

**decease,** death.
**disease,** illness, ailment.

**diner,** one who is dining.
**dinner,** the midday or evening meal.
**donor,** a giver.

**efficient,** able to do good work.
**efficacious,** able to produce the intended effect.

**factor,** a number contained exactly in another number; an agent.
**fracture,** a break.

**fluid,** a liquid, that which flows.
**fluent,** flowing.

**honourable,** worthy of honour, illustrious.
**honorary,** holding office without pay.

**human,** pertaining to mankind.
**humane,** tender, merciful.

**imperial,** belonging to an empire.
**imperious,** haughty, commanding.

**isolate,** to place by itself.
**insulate,** to separate by a non-conductor.

**legible,** readable.
**eligible,** worthy to be chosen, desirable.

**luxuriant,** growing richly.
**luxurious,** providing luxury.

**minster,** a church (abbey).
**minister,** a clergyman, a member of the Cabinet.

**mythical,** relating to myth or fable, untrue.
**mystical,** relating to mystery, involving a sacred or secret meaning.

**necessary,** something that cannot be done without.
**necessity,** something that is unavoidable.

**observation,** act of observing, a remark.
**observance,** the keeping of a rule or custom.

**officer,** a person entrusted with command.
**official,** a subordinate public servant.

**peruse,** to read.
**pursue,** to follow.

**poplar,** a tree.
**popular,** enjoying the favour of the people.

**pretext,** excuse, pretended reason.
**precept,** a rule of conduct.

**raiment,** clothing.
**remnant,** anything left.

**receipt,** act of receiving, document acknowledging receipt of goods or money.
**recipe,** a list of ingredients and operations in cookery.

**register,** book containing a list of names. **registry,** act of registering; a registrar's office.
**registrar,** person who keeps a register.

**sculptor,** a worker in stone.
**sculpture,** a sculptor's work.

**specimen,** an example, sample.
**species,** a kind, subdivision of a genus.

**suburb,** the outskirts of a town.
**superb,** majestic, grand.

**surplice,** a priest's linen vestment.
**surplus,** what is over.

**verger,** a church official.
**verdure,** greenness.

**villain,** a rascal.
**villein,** a baron's feudal follower or dependant.

## 9. SILENT LETTERS

| | |
|---|---|
| a | **parliament, Michael, weapon.** |
| b | **debtor, indebted, subtle, entombed, plumb.** |
| c | **indict, indictment, scythe, victuals, scimitar, descent, rescind.** |
| d | **handsome.** |
| e | **yeoman, sleight.** |
| g | **gnome, impugn, malign, condign, campaign, diaphragm, foreigner.** |
| gh | **fraught.** |
| ugh | **furlough.** |
| h | **ghastly, ghostly, rheumatism, rhinoceros, rhombus.** |
| i | **heifer, leisurely, plait, plaid.** |
| k | **knell, knickerbocker, knighthood, knout, Knieper.** |
| l | **salmon, qualm, qualmish, almond.** |
| n | **kiln, column.** |
| o | **jeopardy, leopard.** |
| p | **contempt, exempt, cupboard, pneumonia, pneumatic, psalm, psalmist.** |
| s | **aisle, viscount.** |
| t | **Christmas, chestnut, waistcoat, mortgage.** |
| th | **asthmatic.** |

22

| u  | **circuit, conduit, biscuit, gauge.** |
|----|----|
| ue | **harang**ue, **colleag**ue, **morg**ue, **plag**ue. |
| w  | **playwright, untoward,** wreath, wreathe, wrangler, wrestler. |

## 10. HOMONYMS

| alter<br>altar | You will **alter** as you grow older.<br>The **altar** is at the east end of the church. |
|---|---|
| ascent<br>assent | The coach passengers walked up this **ascent.**<br>Will you give your **assent** to the proposal? |
| bazaar<br>bizarre | I bought this shawl at a **bazaar.**<br>What a **bizarre** (odd) costume to wear! |
| border<br>boarder | Please keep off the grass **border.**<br>I am a **boarder** in that house. |
| Britain<br>Briton | Great **Britain** is an island.<br>A **Briton** is an inhabitant of **Britain.** |
| burrow<br>borough | The rabbit lives in a **burrow.**<br>The mayor of the **borough** opened the new hospital. |
| canon<br>cannon | He was made a **canon** of the cathedral.<br>The **cannon** went off with a loud report. |
| canvas<br>canvass | Sails are made of stout **canvas.**<br>Did you **canvass** for votes at the election? |
| ceiling<br>sealing | The **ceiling** of the chamber was ornamented.<br>I fastened the letter with **sealing**-wax. This island was once a **sealing** ground. |
| compliment<br>complement | Do you intend that as a **compliment?**<br>The ship had its full **complement** of men. |
| council<br>counsel | The **council** meets monthly.<br>The wise man gave good **counsel.** |
| dependant (n.)<br>dependent (adj.) | The servant was his master's **dependant.**<br>We are all **dependent** on others for something. |

| | |
|---|---|
| **disease** | This **disease** is incurable. |
| **decease** | His **decease** (death) was unexpected. |
| **licence** (n.) | I have paid for a fishing **licence.** |
| **license** (v.) | The borough council will **license** you as a hawker. |
| **manner** | I did not like the gentleman's **manner.** |
| **manor** | I discovered that he was lord of the **manor.** |
| **marshal** | The general began to **marshal** (arrange) his men. |
| **martial** | Cowards often have a **martial** (military) bearing. |
| **muscle** | Regular exercise strengthens one's **muscle.** |
| **mussel** | **Mussel**-shells are found on the sea-shore. |
| **pedal** | The bicycle has a **pedal** for each foot. |
| **peddle** | Hawkers **peddle** goods. |
| **pendant** | A **pendant** is a lady's ornament. |
| **pendent** | The dew-drops hung **pendent** from the boughs. |
| **practice** (n.) | **Practice** makes perfect. |
| **practise** (v.) | **Practise** your scales every day. |
| **principle** (n.) | This is a good **principle** (rule of conduct) to act upon. |
| **principal** (n. adj.) | The college **principal** is one of the **principal** citizens. |
| **valley** | The two hills were separated by a wide **valley.** |
| **valet** | A **valet** is a gentleman's personal servant. |

# 11. DERIVATION

## COMPOUND WORDS

*Note that some compound words are written with a hyphen, others without.*

*Compound nouns formed of:*

1. Noun + noun: **carriage-lamp, thunder-cloud, water-bottle, shopkeeper, fire-guard, oil-can, pancake,**

**pigsty, railway, churchyard, shoehorn, witchcraft.**

2. Verb + noun: **breakfast, looking-glass, grindstone, toasting-fork, laughing-stock, kneading-trough.**
3. Adjective + Noun: **half-back, main-deck, hot-head, freeman.**
4. Adverb + verb: **intake, outcome, farewell, back-wash.**
5. Phrases: **commander-in-chief, rat-a-tat, man-of-war, forget-me-not, hide-and-seek, give-and-take.**

*Compound adjectives formed of:*

1. Noun + Adjective: **week-old, sky-blue, milk-white, air-tight, homesick, top-heavy, blameworthy, sea-green, fire-proof.**
2. Noun + verb: **pigheaded, zinc-lined, ink-stained, psalm-singing, heart-rending, blood-curdling, earth-shaking, moth-eaten, heart-broken.**
3. Adjective + noun: **high-pressure, fresh-water, deep-sea.**
4. Adjective + verb: **old-fashioned, cold-blooded, bad-tempered, savage-looking, hollow-cheeked, thin-skinned, sad-faced.**
5. Adjective + adjective: **red-hot, dark-blue, lukewarm.**
6. Preposition + noun: **overseas.**

*Compound verbs formed of:*

1. Noun + verb: **hoodwink, hamstring, waylay, browbeat.**
2. Adverb, adjective or preposition + verb: **oversew, outdo, whitewash, overreach, oversee, dumbfound.**

*Compound adverbs formed of:*

1. Noun + noun: **sideways, lengthways.**
2. Noun + adjective: **headlong.**
3. Phrases: **by and by, by the by.**

# ENGLISH PREFIXES

**a** = on, in: **ashore** (on shore), **asleep, afloat**.

**a** = of, off, up: **anew, alight, awake**.

**after** = behind, later: **afternoon, afterwards, afterthought**.

**be, by** = by, near to, to make: **beside, by-path, benumb, befriend**.

**for** = from, away, utterly, without: **forbid** (to bid from), **forswear** (to swear from, deny), **forlorn** (utterly lost).

**fore** = before: **foresee** (to see beforehand), **forehead, forewarn, forenoon**.

**gain** = against: **gainsay** (to say against).

**in (en, em)** = in, to make: **inlet, inmate, inland, entwine, enrich, embitter**.

**mis** = ill, wrong: **misdeed, misbehave, misplace, mislead, misjudge**.

**n** = not: **never, neither, nor, naught**.

**out** = beyond: **outlaw, outrun, outlive, outpost, outhouse**.

**over** = beyond: **oversight, overflow, overcoat, overeat**.

**thorough** = through: **thoroughfare, thoroughbred**.

**to** = the or this: **today, tomorrow, tonight, toward**.

**twi** = double: **twilight, twin, twice**.

**un** = opposite to: **unripe, untruth, untold, untidy**.

**un** = reversal of action: **unlearn, undo, untie**.

**under** = beneath: **underground, undergo, undersell**.

**up** = up: **uphold, upright, upstart**.

**with** = back, against: **withhold, withdraw, withstand**.

# ENGLISH SUFFIXES

*Forming nouns:*

(*a*) Denoting person or agent:

**man** = a person: **woman, storeman, fisherman**.

**monger** = a dealer: **fishmonger, ironmonger**.

**wife** = a woman: **housewife, fishwife**.

**wright** = workman: **wheelwright, shipwright**.

**er, ier, yer, ar, or** = male agent: **fighter, talker, collier, hosier, sawyer, lawyer, liar, sailor.**

**son, ing** = son of: **Smithson, king.**

(*b*) Diminutive suffixes, denoting something smaller:

**le, el**: **icicle, bundle, satchel. en: maiden, chicken.**

**kin**: **mannikin, lambkin, napkin.**

**ling**: **darling, fondling, duckling.**

**ock**: **hillock, hammock, bullock.**

**et**: **floweret, floret.**

(*c*) Other noun suffixes:

**craft** = skill: **handicraft, woodcraft, bookcraft.**

**dom** = state: **freedom, kingdom, earldom, wisdom.**

**hood** = state: **childhood, boyhood, neighbourhood.**

**ship** = state, quality: **hardship, friendship, generalship.**

**ness** = state, feeling: **darkness, kindness, tenderness, weakness.**

*Forming verbs:*

(*a*) Causing or making:

**en, n**: **brighten, ripen, frighten, glisten, hasten, own, drown.**

**se**: **cleanse.**

**le**: **startle, curdle.**

(*b*) Repeated action:

**er, le**: **chatter, rattle, cackle.**

*Forming adverbs:*

(*a*) Manner:

**ly**: **wisely, happily, wickedly.**

**wise**: **nowise, crosswise, otherwise, likewise.**

**ling, long**: **darkling, headlong.**

**way, ways**: **always, anyway, straightway.**

(*b*) Place or direction:

**ward, wards**: **backward, downward, seaward, homewards.**

(c) Time:

**om: seldom.**
**er: ever, never.**
**n: then, when.**

*Forming adjectives:*

(a) Possession of quality:

**ey, y: clayey, cloudy, stony.**
**ful: hopeful, faithful, handful.**
**ish: brownish, foolish, feverish.**
**like, ly: womanly, god-like, sickly, heavenly, kindly.**
**some: lonesome, quarrelsome, wearisome, toothsome.**
**less** = without: **fearless, ceaseless, luckless, guiltless.**

(b) Other suffixes:

**en** = made of: **wooden, woollen, oaten, golden, earthen, leathern.**
**ed** = with, possessed of: **gifted.**
**ern** = direction: **eastern, western, northern, southern.**

## NEGATIVE PREFIXES

*Owing to the demands of euphony (pleasing sound) the **n** of **in** often changes according to the consonant that follows.*

**in (ig, il, im, ir)** = not: **indocile, insensible, infamous** (wicked), **innocuous, indecent, intractable, ignoble, illogical, illegible, impossible, improvident, immovable, irreverent, irresolute, irresponsible, irrespective.**
**un** = not: **unable, unsteady, unstable, unnecessary, unacceptable, unfamiliar, uninhabitable.**
**dis** = not: **disagreeable, discontinue, disloyal, dissatisfy, disobliging.**

## 12. BEGINNINGS OR ENDINGS ALIKE

para      parallel, parapet, paradise, paragraph.

ary      stationary, secondary, dictionary.

ain      ascertain, entertain, maintain.

eer      privateer, pioneer, profiteer, gazetteer.

ine (pron. **in**) feminine, masculine, medicine, determine, sanguine.

ine (pron. **een**) vaseline, quarantine.

ite (pron. **it**) exquisite, hypocrite, definite, infinite, favourite.

ite (as in **bite**) cordite, expedite, despite.

tion      application, installation, habitation, assertion, ambition, education, attention, argumentation, invitation.

gue      morgue, league, colleague

sion     ⎱
cion     ⎰ expulsion, omission, emulsion, suspicion.

cle      article, particle, pinnacle, spectacle, miracle.

ment      implement, statement, judgement, reinforcement, tournament, government.

ile      juvenile, infantile, puerile.

ive (pron. **iv**) native, motive, missive, sensitive, explosive, positive.

ism      socialism, organism.

eous      courageous, hideous, erroneous, advantageous, piteous, plenteous.

uous      strenuous, conspicuous.

ous      frivolous, pious, momentous.

ude      latitude, longitude, magnitude, servitude, decrepitude.

ule      ridicule, molecule.

ally      accidentally, mortally, confidentially, nonsensically.

# 13. ETYMOLOGY OF NAMES OF PLACES

**aber** (Celtic) a confluence: **Aberdeen, Aberystwyth.**

**avon** (Celtic) a river: **Avonmouth.**

**beck** (Scandinavian) a brook: **Holbeck.**

**burn** (Scottish) a brook: **Blackburn, Tyburn.**

**burgh** (Teutonic) a fortified place: **Edinburgh.**

**by** (Scandinavian) a dwelling: **Derby, Rugby, Whitby.**

**caster, cester, chester** (Latin) a camp: **Lancaster, Leicester, Winchester.**

**coln** (Latin) a colony: **Lincoln.**

**den** or **dean** (Teutonic) a wooded valley: **Tenterden, Hazeldean.**

**dum** or **dun** (Gaelic) hill fortress: **Dumbarton, Dunmore.**

**esk** (Gaelic) water: **Esk, Exeter.**

**field** (Teutonic) plain: **Huddersfield, Lichfield.**

**fell** (Norse) a mountain: **Snaefell, Scawfell.**

**folk** (Anglo-Saxon) people: **Norfolk, Suffolk.**

**gate** (Teutonic) a passage: **Reigate, Canongate.**

**ham** (Anglo-Saxon) a home: **Birmingham, Buckingham.**

**hithe** (Anglo-Saxon) a haven: **Greenhithe, Hythe.**

**hurst** (Anglo-Saxon) a wood: **Lyndhurst, Sandhurst.**

**innis** or **ennis** (Celtic) an island: **Enniskillen.**

**inver** (Gaelic) mouth of a river: **Inverness.**

**linn** (Celtic) a waterfall: **Roslin, Linlithgow.**

**llan** (Welsh) a church: **Llandaff.**

**low** (Anglo-Saxon) a rising ground: **Ludlow, Hounslow.**

**mere** or **moor** (Anglo-Saxon) lake or marsh: **Windermere, Mersey.**

**minster** (Anglo-Saxon) monastic foundation: **Westminster.**

**ness** (Scandinavian) a nose: **Dungeness, Caithness.**

**pont** (Latin) a bridge: **Pontefract.**

**ross, ros** (Celtic) a promontory: **Kinross, Roscommon.**

**scar** (Scandinavian) a cliff: **Scarborough.**

**set** (Anglo-Saxon) a seat: **Dorset, Somerset.**

**sex** (Anglo-Saxon) Saxons: **Essex, Sussex.**

**stead** (Anglo-Saxon) a town: **Hampstead.**
**street** (Latin) a Roman road: **Street, Streatham.**
**thorpe** (Norse) a village: **Heythorpe.**
**toft** (Danish) an enclosure: **Lowestoft.**
**tor** (Celtic) a tall rock: **Torbay, Kintore.**
**wick** (Anglo-Saxon) a village: **Berwick, Warwick.**
**worth** (Anglo-Saxon) a farm: **Tamworth, Worthing.**

## 14. ANTONYMS (OR OPPOSITES)

### Nouns

| | | | |
|---|---|---|---|
| tele'scope | mi'croscope | friend'ly | hos'tile |
| en'trance | ex'it | plus | mi'nus |
| volunteer' | con'script | inter'nal | exter'nal |
| mi'ser | spend'thrift | mas'culine | fem'inine |
| anal'ysis | syn'thesis | con'vex | con'cave |
| nu'merator | denom'inator | na'tive | for'eign |
| expan'sion | contrac'tion | lay | cler'ical |
| debt'or | cred'itor | cour'teous | discour'teous |
| major'ity | minor'ity | conspic'uous | inconspic'uous |
| dexter'ity | awk'wardness | sep'tic | antisep'tic |
| accep'tance | refus'al | le'gal | ille'gal |
| scarc'ity | abun'dance | le'nient | mer'ciless |
| vig'our | decrep'itude | vig'orous | decrep'it |
| evapora'tion | condensa'tion | transpar'ent | opaque' |

### Adjectives

### Verbs

| | | | |
|---|---|---|---|
| inhale' | exhale' | wax | wane |
| invig'orate | en'ervate | has'ten | loi'ter |
| attract' | repel' | refresh' | exhaust' |
| increase' | decrease' | im'prison | release' |
| tight'en | relax' | evap'orate | condense' |

# 15. WORDS GROUPED ACCORDING TO MEANING

*A token list to which pupils may add their own words.*

| | |
|---|---|
| Birds | **petrel.** |
| Animals | **alpaca, camelopard, chameleon, chimpanzee, giraffe, rhinoceros, hippopotamus.** |
| Trees | **acacia, eucalptus, cypress.** |
| Flowers | **camellia, nasturtium, chrysanthemum, salvia, dahlia, fuchsia, geranium, polyanthus.** |
| Vegetables | **asparagus, broccoli, celery, spinach.** |
| Diseases or ailments | **bronchitis, catarrh, diarrhoea, diphtheria, dysentery, dyspepsia, pleurisy, pneumonia, neuralgia, appendicitis, rheumatism.** |
| Drugs | **penicillin, cocaine, strychnine.** |
| Insect life | **cochineal, chrysalis, cocoon.** |
| Condiments | **cinnamon, caraway, dessicated coconut.** |
| Physiology | **diaphragm, vertebra, biceps, aorta, venous** |
| Musical instruments | **violin, cello, saxophone, oboe, clarinet.** |
| Figures of speech | **simile, metaphor, irony, personification.** |
| Grammar | **conjunction, preposition, interjection, positive, comparative, superlative, nominative, possessive, objective, subject, predicate, object, relative, antecedent, participle.** |

# 16. WORD-BUILDING GROUPS

| | | | |
|---|---|---|---|
| **do'cile** | **assass'in** | **withhold'** | **na'tion** |
| **do'cilely** | **assass'inate** | **withhold'ing** | **na'tional** |
| **docil'ity** | **assassina'tion** | **withheld'** | **national'ity** |
| **col'ony** | **col'onize** | **sim'ilar** | **propose'** |
| **col'onist** | **col'onizer** | **similar'ity** | **propo'sal** |
| **colo'nial** | **coloniz'ation** | **dissim'ilar** | **proposi'tion** |

| | | | |
|---|---|---|---|
| exceed′ | rogue | con′fident | effect′ |
| exceed′ingly | ro′guish | con′fidence | effec′tive |
| excess′ | ro′guery | confiden′tial | ineffec′tive |
| excess′ive | ro′guishly | confiden′tially | effec′tual |

| | | | |
|---|---|---|---|
| vil′lain | base | soci′ety | distin′guish |
| vil′lainous | ba′sis | so′cial | distin′guishable |
| vil′lainy | debase′ | so′ciable | indistin′guishable |

| | | | |
|---|---|---|---|
| mim-ic | pic′nic | frol′ic | biv′ouac |
| mim′icking | pic′nicking | frol′icking | biv′ouacking |
| mim′icked | pic′nicked | frol′icked | biv′ouacked |

| | | | |
|---|---|---|---|
| devel′op | cel′ebrate | invest′igate | elect′ |
| devel′oper | cel′ebrates | invest′igating | elect′ion |
| devel′oping | cel′ebrating | invest′igated | elect′or |
| devel′oped | cel′ebrated | investiga′tion | elect′oral |
| devel′opment | celebra′tion | invest′igator | elect′ive |

| | | | |
|---|---|---|---|
| athlet′ic | den′tal | superintend′ | pronounce′ |
| athlet′ics | den′tist | superinten′dent | pronounce′able |
| ath′lete | dent′istry | superinten′dence | pronuncia′tion |

| | | | |
|---|---|---|---|
| exhib′it | dimin′ish | advise′ | suggest′ |
| exhib′itor | dimin′utive | advis′able | sugges′tion |
| exhibi′tion | diminu′tion | inadvis′able | sugges′tive |

| | | | |
|---|---|---|---|
| pop′ular | agree′ | spec′ial | ad′vertise |
| popular′ity | agree′ment | spec′ially | ad′vertising |
| pop′ulous | disagree′ment | special′ity | ad′vertised |
| pop′ulate | agree′able | espec′ial | ad′vertiser |
| popula′tion | disagree′able | espec′ially | adver′tisement |

| | | | |
|---|---|---|---|
| sep′arate | for′tune | crit′ic | conve′nient |
| separa′tion | misfor′tune | crit′ical | conve′niently |
| sep′arator | for′tunate | crit′icism | conve′nience |
| insep′arable | unfor′tunate | critique′ | inconve′nience |

| | | | |
|---|---|---|---|
| consid′er | sincere′ | cer′emony | mul′tiply |
| considera′tion | sincere′ly | cer′emonies | multiplica′tion |
| consid′erable | sincer′ity | ceremon′ious | multiplic′ity |
| inconsid′erable | insincere′ | ceremon′ial | mul′tiple |

plas'tic      ac'cident       cit'y          fi'nal
plastic'ity   accident'al     cit'izen       fi'nally
plas'ticine   accident'ally   cit'izenship   final'ity
per'iod       em'pire         rid'icule      mys'tery
period'ical   imper'ial       ridic'ulous    myster'ious
excite'       endow'          hos'tile       in'dustry
excit'able    endowed'        hos'tilely     indus'trial
excitabil'ity endow'ment      hostil'ity     indus'trious
nov'el        con'science     immense'       proph'et
nov'elty      conscien'tious  immens'ity     prophet'ic
tres'pass     compete'        ju'bilate      compare'
tres'passes   compet'ing      ju'bilant      compar'ative
tres'passers  competi'tion    ju'bilance     compar'atively
tres'passed   compet'itor     ju'bilee*      compar'ison
au'thor       provide'        prime          civ'il
au'thoress    provis'ion      pri'mary       civil'ian
author'ity    prov'ident      prim'itive     civ'ilize
au'thorize    prov'idence     prem'ier       civiliza'tion
extend'       conspire'       pub'lish       co-op'erate
exten'sion    conspir'ator    pub'lisher     co-opera'tion
extens'ive    conspir'acy     pub'lishable   co-op'erative
ur'ban        respect'        precise'       commit'
sub'urb       respect'ive     precise'ly     commit'tee
subur'ban     respect'ively   precis'ion     commis'sion
assure'       mor'al          prof'it        impede'
assured'      mor'ally        profiteer'     imped'iment
assur'ance    moral'ity       prof'itable    impediment'a
pub'lic       in'dicate       volunteer'     iden'tity
pub'lican     in'dicator      vol'untary     iden'tical
publica'tion  in'dicatory     vol'untarily   iden'tify
public'ity    indic'ative     invol'untary   identifica'tion
coal          condemn'        hyp'ocrite     ad'equate
col'lier      condem'natory   hypocrit'ical  ade'quacy
col'liery     condemna'tion   hypoc'risy     inad'equate

*Not derived from **jubilate**.

# PART TWO

## 1. REVISION OF SPELLING RULES

*Final consonant doubled before a vowel:*

| | | | |
|---|---|---|---|
| abhorring | abhorred | panelling | panelled |
| debarring | debarred | enamelling | enamelled |
| modelling | modelled | incurring | incurred |
| labelling | labelled | acquitting | acquitted |
| crystallizing | crystallized | remitting | remitted |

*Final consonant not doubled:*

| | | | |
|---|---|---|---|
| banqueting | banqueted | pivoting | pivoted |
| limiting | limited | applauding | applauded |
| summoning | summoned | prevailing | prevailed |
| assailing | assailed | retailing | retailed |

*Final* **e** *dropped, mostly before vowel suffixes:*

| | | | |
|---|---|---|---|
| persecuting | persecuted | superseding | superseded |
| prosecuting | prosecuted | interceding | interceded |
| criticizing | criticized | reconciling | reconciled |
| conceivable | incorrigibly | translatable | reconcilable |
| insensible | profanity | preceding | preceded |
| innovation | divinity | perversity | paralyzing |
| authorizing | excitability | scrutinizing | scrutinized |
| operative | inoperative | opportunity | mobilized |
| pleasurable | immeasurably | indescribable | spherical |

*Final* **e** *retained, mostly before consonantal suffixes:*

| | | |
|---|---|---|
| indefinitely | comparatively | outrageous |
| rateable | acreage | resolutely |
| plaintively | prematurely | vindictively |
| appropriateness | advantageous | postponement |

*Final* **y** *changed to* **i**:   *Final* **y** *retained:*

| | | | |
|---|---|---|---|
| memorial | ordinarily | necessarily | verifying |
| testimonial | embodiment | burglarious | mystifying |
| ceremonial | mystification | worthily | justifying |
| luxurious | moodily | temporarily | horrifying |

*Final* **y** *dropped:*

| | | | |
|---|---|---|---|
| calamitous | mutinous | sorcerer | necessitous |

*Use of prefixes* **dis-** *and* **mis-**:

| | | | |
|---|---|---|---|
| dispossess | dissentient | misappropriate | |
| disintegrate | dissolute | mis-statement | mishap |
| discussion | dissatisfaction | misinterpret | mis-shapen |

*Some double consonants:*

| | | | |
|---|---|---|---|
| accommodate | assassinate | succinct | vicissitude |
| exaggerate | aggressive | commemorate | annihilate |
| irrigate | irresolute | asseverate | commandeer |
| accessible | incurred | commissioner | suffocate |
| association | sufficiency | communicate | aggregate |

## 2. SYLLABIFICATION AND ACCENTUATION

*(See introductory note on page* 16)

*Accent on first syllable:*

| | | | |
|---|---|---|---|
| ap'-pli-ca-ble | in'-ven-to-ry | col'-leagues | prel'-ude |
| ad'-mir-al-ty | con'-verse | sup'-pli-cate | cur'-so-ry |

| | | | |
|---|---|---|---|
| rep´-u-ta-ble | al´-ka-li | im´-pli-cate | fal´-la-cy |
| rep´-ar-a-ble | an´-ar-chist | du´-pli-cate | sol´-u-ble |
| rep´-li-ca | en´-er-vate | im´-pi-ous | ver´-i-fy |
| per´-emp-to-ry | lam´-ent-a-ble | rhet´-o-ric | ob´-se-quies |
| cas´-ual-ties | ter´-min-a-ble | in´-tri-ca-cy | ex´-o-dus |
| con´-tro-ver-sy | sed´-a-tive | ret´-i-cent | ar´-ti-fice |
| ex´-pe-dite | prej´-u-dice | sed´-en-ta-ry | pre´-cincts |
| mem´-or-a-ble | lu´-cra-tive | rev´-er-ie | cou´-pon |
| min´-i-a-ture | gar´-ru-lous | prem´-i-ses | lig´-a-ture |
| ul´-ti-mate-ly | prow´-ess | cou´-ri-er | cor´-o-ner |
| dio´-o-cese | vac´-u-um | sub´-ju-gate | an´-ti-qua-ted |
| pre´-mi-um | des´pic-a-ble | al´-ter-nate | ap´-ti-tude |
| in´-fa-mous | des´-ic-ca-ted | syc´-a-more | der´-e-lict |
| ve´-he-ment | com´-ment | des´-e-crate | trel´-lised |
| om´-in-ous | suf´-frage | ad´-ju-tant | mel´-an-chol-y |
| on´-er-ous | scal´-a-wag | prel´-ate | du´-bi-ous |

*Accent on second syllable:*

| | | |
|---|---|---|
| in-gre´-di-ents | in-ter´-sti-ces | pro-pri´-e-ty |
| ir-rep´-ar-able | e-lu´-ci-date | ap-pro´-pri-ate |
| i-mag´-i-nary | in-sen´-sate | per-sua´-sive |
| au-rif´-er-ous | syn-op´-sis | pro-phet´-ic |
| pre-rog´-a-tive | pa-ral´-y-sis | an-al´-o-gy |
| fan-at´-ic | e-nu´-mer-ate | u-nan´-i-mous |
| her-ed´-i-ta-ry | in-ter´-min-a-ble | be-la´-ted |
| per-im´-e-ter | in-ev´-i-ta-ble | o-blit´-er-ate |
| im-plac´-a-ble | as-bes´-tos | pre-sen´-ti-ment |
| in-com´-par-a-ble | e-lim´-in-ate | su-prem´-a-cy |
| ex-ec´-u-tive | an-at´-o-my | ap-par´-el |
| ex-ec´-u-tor | in-dem´-ni-ty | in-vest´-ment |
| in-cen´-sed | de-cid´-u-ous | mu-ni´-ci-pal |
| ben-ev´-o-lence | con-temp´-or-ar-y | de-gen´-er-ate |
| com-mem´-or-ate | dis-con´-so-late | cru-sade |
| de-riv´-a-tive | so-lil´-o-quy | ob-se´-qui-ous |
| phil-an´-thro-pist | an-tip´-o-des | in-ter´-pre-ter |
| a-cum´-en | re-cip´-ro-cal | ma-lign´ |

| | | |
|---|---|---|
| ben-e-dic'-tion | pen-i-ten'-ti-ar-y | man-u-fac'-ture |
| cen-tri-fu'-gal | cor-o-na'-tion | ge-o-graph'-i-cal |
| ig-no-min'-i-ous | mer-i-tor'-i-ous | prov-o-ca'-tion |
| ren-o-va'-tion | ir-re-triev'-a-ble | the-or-et'-i-cal |
| con-sign-ee' | con-tig-u'-i-ty | mign-on-ette' |
| rep-re-sen'-ta-tive | ge-ne-al'-o-gy | su-per-cil'-i-ous |
| arch-i-tec'-tur-al | rev-o-lu'-tion-ize | cor-nu-co'-pi-a |
| leg-is-la'-tion | pe-ri-od'-i-cal | ef-fi-ca'-cious |
| ep-i-dem'-ic | su-perflu-'i-ty | re-qui-si'-tion |

*Accent on fourth syllable:*

| | | |
|---|---|---|
| pro-nun-ci-a'-tion | Med-i-ter-ra'-ne-an | col-on-i-za'-tion |
| co-op-er-a'-tion | con-cil-i-a'-tion | dis-ci-plin-ar'-i-an |
| pe-cu-li-ar'-i-ty | fa-mil-i-ar'-i-ty | as-so-ci-a'-tion |

# 3. DERIVATION

## LATIN PREFIXES

*Note that a prefix often assimilates itself to (or makes itself like) the beginning of the stem to which it is attached.*

**a, ab, abs** = from, away: **avert,** to turn away; **absolute,** free from control; **absurd,** away from sense; **abstract,** to draw away; **abbreviate,** to shorten from (see **ad**).

**ad (a, ab, ac, af, ag, al, an, ap, ar, as, at)** = to: **adhere,** to stick to; **ascend,** to climb to; **accept,** to take, to receive; **afflict,** to give pain or grief to; **aggravate,** to give weight to; **arrive,** to come or go to, reach; **attain,** reach to; **abbreviate.**

**ante, anti*** = before: **antecedent,** going before; **anticipate,** to see before, expect; **antique.**

**bene** = well: **benefit,** a kindness, a favour; **benediction,** a saying well, a blessing; **beneficent,** well-doing, generous.

*Contrast with Greek prefix *anti* on page 43.

**circum** = round about: **circumference,** bounding line; **circuit,** distance round about; **circuitous, circumvent.**

**con (co, col, com, cog, cor)** = with: **connect,** to tie with, join; **co-operate,** to work with; **collect,** to put with, gather; **cognate,** born with, akin; **correspond,** agree with, communicate with.

**contra, counter** = against: **contradict,** to say against, deny; **counterbalance,** weigh against; **counterpoise.**

**de** = down, away from: **defend,** to ward off; **descend,** to climb down.

**dis, dif** = apart, away: **dismantle,** to take down; **dismount,** to get off a horse; **diffuse,** to spread.

**ex (e, ef, ec)** = off, out: **except,** to take out; **emit,** to send out; **effect,** outcome or result; **eccentric,** out of the centre, odd.

**in (en, em, il, ir)** = into, before a verb: **induce,** to lead into, persuade; **invade,** to march into; **enter,** to go into; **illuminate,** to give light into, to light up; **incision,** cut, gash, or act of cutting into; **irradiate, impel, immerse, irritate.**

**in (ig, il, im, ir)** = not, before an adjective: **ignoble,** not noble, mean; **infirm,** not strong, weak; **illegal,** unlawful; **invaluable,** cannot be valued, priceless; **illicit.**

**in,** used as an *intensive*: **inebriated,** drunk.

**inter** = between, among: **interrupt,** to break between; **intervene,** to come between; **interstate,** between states; **intellect, interdependence.**

**intro** = within: **introduce,** to lead in, to make known to.

**male, mal** = badly: **malefactor,** an evil doer; **malcontent,** a dissatisfied person; **malevolent.**

**mis** = badly: **mischief,** the doing of harm or evil; **mis- adventure,** an accident; **miscount,** to count wrongly.

**ne, non** = not: **negation,** saying no, denying; **nonsense,** not sense, absurdity; **non-combatant,** not a fighter.

**ob (o, oc, of, op)** = against, in the way of: **omit,** to leave out; **occur,** to run in the way of, to happen; **oppose,** to place against, hinder; **offer,** to bring before; **obviate.**

**pene** = almost: **peninsula,** almost an island.

**per (pel)** through: **perspire,** to emit through the skin, to sweat; **pellucid,** clear right through; **percolate.**

**post** = after: **postpone,** to place after, put off; **post-mortem.**

**pre** = before: **pre-historic,** before historical record; **predecessor.**

**pro (por, pur, pour)** = for, forth, instead of: **pro-German,** for the Germans; **produce,** to bring forth; **pronoun.**

**re** = back, again: **recoil,** to roll or fall back; **react,** to act back, respond to; **rejoin,** to join again, to answer back; **reassemble,** to assemble again; **remit, repel.**

**sub (suc, suf, sug, sup, sum, sus)** = under: **subterranean,** under the earth; **suspend,** to hang under; **succeed,** to follow after; **summons,** a call or order; **sustain,** to hold up.

**trans** = across: **transmit,** to send across; **transatlantic,** across the Atlantic; **transitory,** passing away quickly.

**un** = not: **uncivil,** not civil, rude; **untoward,** awkward, inconvenient.

## LATIN SUFFIXES

*Forming nouns:*

(*a*) Denoting agent or instrument:

| | |
|---|---|
| ado | **desperado,** a desperate fellow; **renegado,** a deserter. |
| age | **savage,** an uncivilized man; **hostage,** one kept as pledge. |
| an | **guardian,** a protector. |
| ain | **chieftain,** a headman, leader; **captain,** an officer. |
| on | **sexton,** a church caretaker; **champion,** a defender. |
| en | **citizen,** a city dweller; **warden,** one in charge. |
| ance | **conveyance,** a means of transport. |
| ant | **merchant,** a trader; **assistant,** a helper. |
| and | **brigand,** a robber. |
| ent | **student,** a learner; **client,** a customer. |

40

| | |
|---|---|
| **ard** | **sluggard,** a lazy person; **drunkard,** one who gets drunk. |
| **art** | **braggart,** one who boasts. |
| **ee** | **trustee,** one trusted to act for another; **devotee,** one zealously devoted to a cause. |
| **ess** | **heiress,** a female heir; **shepherdess,** a female shepherd. |
| **ive** | **fugitive,** one fleeing; **native,** one born in a place. |
| **ic** | **lunatic,** a mad person; **rustic,** a country person. |
| **or** | **actor,** one who acts; **governor,** a ruler. |
| **er** | **robber,** one who robs; **trader,** one who trades. |
| **eer** | **engineer,** one skilled in mechanical construction; **musketeer,** a soldier bearing a musket. |
| **our** | **saviour,** one who saves life. |
| **eur** | **amateur,** a novice, not a professional; **connoisseur,** an expert judge. |

(*b*) Denoting state, condition, office:

| | |
|---|---|
| **age** | **bondage,** state of slavery; **peerage,** the order of peers. |
| **ance** | **repentance,** condition of having repented; **arrogance,** proud behaviour. |
| **ancy** | **brilliancy,** state of brightness. |
| **ency** | **regency,** office of regent. |
| **ence** | **absence,** state of being absent. |
| **ice** | **novice,** a learner; **cowardice,** condition of being a coward. |
| **lence** | **violence,** state of being violent; **insolence,** impertinence. |
| **ment** | **judgement,** act of judging; **payment,** act of paying. |
| **ude** | **gratitude,** state of being grateful. |

(*c*) Diminutives:

| | |
|---|---|
| **cule** | **molecule,** a little drop. |
| **cle** | **particle,** a small part. |
| **et** | **pellet,** a little ball; **eaglet,** a young eagle. |
| **ette** | **cigarette,** a little cigar; **statuette,** a small statue. |
| **let** | **streamlet,** a small stream; **rootlet,** a tiny root. |

**age**    **village,** a small assemblage of houses; **cottage,** a little house.

**ary**    **library,** a room for books; **granary,** a grain-shed.

**ery**    **cemetery,** a burial place; **deanery,** a dean's house.

**ory**    **factory,** a work place; **dormitory,** a sleeping-room.

*Forming adjectives :*

**able**    **arable,** fit for ploughing; **culpable,** blameworthy.

**aceous**    **farinaceous,** containing flour; **herbaceous,** herb-like.

**acious**    **loquacious,** talkative; **mendacious,** lying.

**al**    **poetical,** pertaining to, or like, poetry; **regal,** like a king.

**aneous**    **simultaneous,** happening at the same time; **contemporaneous,** existing at the same time.

**ant**    **vagrant,** wandering; **ignorant,** lacking knowledge.

**ary**    **contrary,** opposite, different; **solitary,** lonely.

**ate**    **passionate,** quick-tempered; **fortunate,** lucky.

**ean**    **subterranean,** beneath the ground; **European,** belonging to Europe.

**esque**    **picturesque,** like a picture, beautiful; **grotesque,** absurd.

**ible**    **horrible,** inspiring horror; **terrible,** inspiring terror.

**id**    **frigid,** very cold; **acid,** sour; **pallid,** pale.

**ile**    **fragile,** very weak; **docile,** tame; **agile,** active.

**ior**    **superior,** higher in rank; **inferior,** lower in rank.

**ite**    **polite,** well-mannered; **contrite,** repentant.

**ive**    **sportive,** playful; **pensive,** thoughtful.

**lent**    **corpulent,** stout; **opulent,** wealthy.

**ous**    **glorious,** noble, splendid; **adventurous,** fond of adventure.

**uble**    **soluble,** able to be dissolved.

**ute**    **absolute,** free from control; **minute,** very small.

*Forming verbs:*

| | |
|---|---|
| **ate** | **captivate,** to make captive; **agitate,** to disturb greatly. |
| **esce** | **coalesce,** to unite; **acquiesce,** to assent to. |
| **fy** | **magnify,** to make large; **simplify,** to make simple. |
| **ish** | **finish,** to make an end of; **nourish,** to feed. |
| **ite** | ⎱ **ignite,** to set alight; **expedite,** to hasten. |
| **it** | ⎰ **merit,** to deserve. |

# GREEK PREFIXES

**a, an, am** = not, without: **anarchy,** without rule; **anonymous,** without name; **apathy,** without feeling, lack of interest.

**amphi** = about, both: **amphitheatre,** arena with seats around it; **amphibious,** living on land and in water.

**ana, an** = up: **analyse,** to loosen up, separate into parts.

**anti, ant\*** = against; **antipathy,** dislike; **Antarctic,** opposed to Arctic; **antiseptic,** preventing decay; **antipodes.**

**apo, aph** = from: **apology,** a speaking from, an excuse; **apostle,** one sent from, a teacher; **aphorism,** a brief, pithy saying.

**arch, archi** = chief: **archbishop,** chief bishop; **architect,** a designer; **archipelago,** lit. chief sea (sea studded with islands).

**auto** = self: **autograph,** signature; **autobiography,** story of one's own life; **automobile,** a motor car.

**cata, cath** = down, throughout: **cataract,** a waterfall; **catholic,** universal; **catapult, catastrophe.**

**dia** = two, through: **diameter,** measurement through; **dialogue,** conversation between two; **dialect, diagram.**

**dis, di** = in two: **dissyllable,** word of two syllables; **dilemma,** a difficult choice or a trying situation.

---

\*Distinguish from Latin prefix *ante.* See page 38.

**dys** = ill: **dyspepsia,** indigestion; **dysentery,** painful diarrhoea.

**ec, ex** = out of: **ecstasy,** rapture; **exorcise,** to drive out an evil spirit.

**en, em** = in: **embed,** to fix in; **enslave,** to bring into slavery.

**epi, eph** = upon: **epigram,** a pithy saying; **ephemeral,** short-lived.

**eso** = within: **esoteric,** secret, opposed to *exoteric.*

**exo** = without: **exoteric,** external, open; **exotic,** from a foreign country.

**eu** = well: **euphony,** sweet sound; **eulogy,** praise.

**hemi** = half: **hemisphere,** half the globe.

**hepta, hept** = seven: **heptagon,** seven-sided figure; **heptarchy,** seven kingdoms.

**hetero** = different: **heterodox,** heretical; **heterogenous,** dissimilar.

**hexa** = six: **hexagon,** six-sided figure; **hexameter,** verse of six feet.

**homos** = the same: **homonym,** same name; **homogeneous,** same kind.

**hyper** = above: **hypercritical,** over-critical; **hyperbole,** exaggeration.

**hypo** = under: **hypocrite,** a false person.

**meta, meth, met** = after, with, change: **metaphor,** a transference of meaning; **method,** manner of work; **meteor,** shooting star.

**para, par** = beside: **parallel,** beside one another; **paragraph,** a short passage of writing; **parish,** ecclesiastical district.

**penta** = five: **pentagon,** five-sided figure.

**peri** = around: **perimeter,** distance round; **periphrasis,** round-about speech; **periscope.**

**poly** = many: **polysyllabic,** containing many syllables; **Polynesia,** many islands.

**pro** = before: **prologue,** preface or introductory speech, opposed to *epilogue*; **programme,** written notice beforehand.

**syn, sym, syl** = with: **synonym,** word of same meaning; **syntax,** correct arrangement of words; **synthesis,** binding together; **syllable,** letters taken together; **sympathy,** fellow-feeling.

## GREEK SUFFIXES

*Forming nouns:*

(*a*) Denoting agent:

| | |
|---|---|
| ac | **maniac,** a madman; **demoniac,** one possessed with a demon. |
| ant | **giant; elephant.** |
| ast | **enthusiast,** one filled with enthusiasm; **gymnast,** one skilled in physical exercises. |
| et | **prophet; poet; comet.** |
| ic | **critic,** a judge; **cynic,** a morose or surly person. |
| ine | **heroine.** |
| is | **artist; royalist; dramatist.** |
| ite, it | **Israelite; hermit.** |
| ot | **patriot,** a lover of his country; **idiot; zealot,** one full of zeal. |

(*b*) Denoting state:

| | |
|---|---|
| asm | **enthusiasm,** deep interest; **spasm,** sudden pain. |
| ism | **baptism; schism,** separation from the Church. |
| sy | **palsy,** loss of power or feeling. |
| y | **energy; harmony,** agreement. |

(*c*) Denoting arts or sciences:

ic, ics  **logic,** art of reasoning; **music; mathematics.**

(*d*) Diminutive:

isk      **asterisk,** a little star; **obelisk,** a tapering pillar.

(*e*) Miscellaneous:

**ad, ade myriad; decade,** ten years.

**e**        **apostrophe,** sign of omission or possession; **acme,** perfection, highest point.

**m, me programme; telegram,** a writing at a distance.

**oid**        **aneroid,** without fluid (of barometers); **negroid; rhomboid.**

**tre**        **centre; metre; sceptre.**

*Forming verbs:*

**ise, ize baptise, baptize; civilise, civilize.**

*Forming adjectives:*

**astic bombastic,** from bombast, high-sounding talk.

**ic**        **graphic,** vividly descriptive; **despotic,** having absolute power.

**istic**        **artistic,** appealing to an artist, beautiful; **eulogistic,** giving praise.

## ENGLISH ROOTS

**bacan** = to bake: **baker, Baxter, batch.**

**bana** = death: **bane, baneful, henbane.**

**beodan** = to command: **bid, beadle** (formerly a parish officer).

**beorgan** = to protect, hide, keep: **borough, burgh, burgher, burgess, burgage, burglar, bury, burial, burrow, harbour.**

**beran** = to bear: **bear, burden, bier, barrow** (handcart).

**bindan** = to tie: **bind, band, bandage, bandog, bond, bondage, bondsman, bundle, woodbine.**

**buan** = to dwell, till: **boor, bondage, bower, byre** (cowshed), **husband, neighbour.**

**bugan** = to bend, bow: **bow, bow-window, elbow, bight, bough, bay, buxom.**

**cunnan** = to know, to be able: **can, con, cunning, ken, canny, uncouth.**

**cyn** = race: **kind, kin, kindred, king.**

**daeg** = day: **day, daisy, dawn.**

**don** = to do: **do, don, doff, deed.**

**dragan** = to draw: **draw, drag, draggle, draught, drawl, dray, drain, dregs, dredge.**

**faran** = to go: **fare, ford, ferry, farewell, thoroughfare.**

**fedan** = to feed: **feed, food, foster.**

**feon** = to hate: **fiend, foe, feud.**

**galan** = to sing: **nightingale.**

**hal** = sound, whole: **hale, whole, wholesome, heal, health, healthy, hail, wassail, holy, holiday, hollyhock, hallow.**

**sceran** = to cut, separate: **scarce, scarify, score, share, shear, shore.**

**slahan** (slagan) = to strike, slay: **slay, slaughter, sledge-hammer.**

**tellan** = tell: **tale, tally, teller, toll.**

**witan** = to know, see: **wit, witness, twit, wise, wisdom, witch, wizard, bewitch, wicked, witanagemot.**

## LATIN ROOTS

*Some examples of word development:*

**facio** (*factus*) = I make, do—*from which we get the following:*

**fact,** a thing done, a reality;

**faction,** taking part, those taking part, a party, a small party;

**factory (manufactory),** a building for the making of goods;

**facile,** easily done (derogatory in meaning);

**facility,** ease in performance, opportunity;

**fashion,** style of dress, customary usage in respect of dress and other things;

**difficulty,** lack of ease in performance;

**effect,** result, influence; to bring about;

**affection,** the state of being affected, or of loving;

**deficient,** not made complete, inadequate, imperfect;

**defect,** the want of something necessary for completeness, imperfection;

**perfection,** the state of being complete, full possession of any desirable quality;

**suffice,** to do or be enough, to satisfy;

**profit,** to make beyond, to gain, to improve, to be of service to;

**gratification,** the act of pleasing, that which affords pleasure;

**feat** (through the French *fait*, done), a thing well done;

**feature** (French, *faiture*), the make, form, shape, or appearance;

**surfeit** (through the French *surfait*), to overdo, eat to excess;

**counterfeit,** to make against, to imitate, especially for a bad purpose;

**feasible** (French, *faisable*), capable of being done, practicable;

**faculty,** ability to perform.


**aequus** = equal: **equality,** state of being equal; **equivalent,** of equal value; **equitable,** fair, just; **iniquity,** wickedness; **adequate,** sufficient; **equilateral, equator, equable.**

**aevum** = age: **coeval,** of same age; **primeval,** ancient.

**ager** = a field: **agriculture,** tilling the fields; **agrarian,** belonging to land.

**ago** (*actus*) = I do or act: **act; actual; agent,** a doer; **agency; agitate,** to disturb; **navigate,** to sail.

**alo** = I flourish, grow: **aliment,** food; **coalition,** a union; **alimentary,** nutritive; **alimony.**

**altus** = high: **altitude,** height; **exalt,** raise; **alto.**

**ambulo** = I walk: **amble,** a slow trot; **perambulator,** a baby's carriage; **ambulance.**

**amo** (*amatus*) = I love: **amiable,** good-tempered; **amorous,** loving; **amity,** friendship; **amateur,** a non-professional, a beginner.

**annus** = a year: **annual,** yearly; **biennial,** every two years; **annals,** historical records; **anniversary,** yearly return of any special day; **perennial,** lasting through the years; **annuity, centennial, triennial.**

**aqua** = water: **aquatic,** pertaining to water; **aqueous,** watery; **aqueduct,** a water channel; **aquarium.**

**arbor** = tree: **arboriculture,** growing of trees, forestry; **arboreal,** living in trees.

**audio** = I hear: **audible,** able to be heard; **audience,** listeners.

**aurum** = gold: **auriferous,** gold-bearing.

**auxilium** = help: **auxiliary,** helping.

**bellum** = war: **rebel,** to fight against; **belligerent,** a nation or party at war, warlike; **bellicose,** quarrelsome; **rebellion.**

**bene** = well, good: **benevolence,** kindness; **benefactor,** one who does good.

**cano** = I sing: **chant,** to sing; **cantata,** a choral work.

**capio** (*captus*) = I take: **captive,** one taken; **accept,** receive.

**caput** (*capitis*) = the head: **capital,** head city; **captain,** head officer; **cape; chapter; decapitate,** behead.

**civis** = a citizen: **civic,** relating to citizens; **civil,** polite; **civilian,** one not a soldier; **city,** a town; **civilize,** to bring out of barbarism.

**ceolum** = heaven: **celestial,** heavenly.

**cognosco** = I ascertain: **recognize,** to know again; **cognizant,** informed of; **incognito,** unknown, in disguise.

**colo** = I till: **colony,** a new settlement; **cultivate,** till; **culture,** act or result of tilling; **agriculture.**

**copia** = plenty: **copious,** plentiful; **copy.**

**coquo** = I boil: **cook; decoction,** extract made by boiling.

**cor** (*cordis*) = heart: **cordial,** hearty; **concord,** agreement (opp. **discord**); **accord, record, courage.**

**corpus** = body: **corpse,** dead body; **corps,** company of soldiers; **corporation.**

**credo** = I believe, trust: **credit,** faith or trust; **creditor,** one to whom money is owing; **creed,** a belief; **credence,** belief; **incredible,** not to be believed;

**credulity,** disposition to believe on slight evidence; **credulous,** too trustful, easily deceived.

**cresco** = I grow: **increase,** to grow larger; **decrease,** to diminish.

**curro** = I run: **current,** running water; **course,** act of running; **concur,** to agree; **incur,** to run into, fall into.

**decem** = ten: **decade,** period of ten years; **December,** formerly the tenth month; **decimate,** to slay every tenth man.

**dico** (*dictus*) = I speak: **diction,** words used; **contradict,** deny; **verdict,** decision of jury; **predict,** foretell.

**dies** = a day: **dial,** clock face; **diary, diurnal.**

**duco** = I lead: **duke,** a noble; **educate,** to teach; **produce,** make.

**eo** (*itus*) = I go: **exit,** going out; **initial,** beginning; **perish,** to die, to suffer destruction.

**facilis** = easy: **facile,** too easy; **facility,** ease; **faculty,** power of mind; **facilitate,** to make easy.

**felix** = happy: **felicity,** happiness; **felicitate,** congratulate.

**fero** (*latus*) = I bear: **fertile,** rich in products; **circumference,** boundary line of circle; **confer,** discuss; **differ,** disagree.

**filius** = son, **filia** = daughter: **filial,** relating to son or daughter.

**finis** = end: **fine,** excellent, sharp; **final,** at an end; **finish,** to end; **finite,** with an end; **definite,** exact; **infinite,** without end.

**flos** = a flower: **floral,** pertaining to flowers; **flora,** the plants of a country; **flourish,** to prosper; **florid.**

**fluo** (*fluxus*) = I flow: **fluent,** ready in the use of words; **fluid,** that which flows; **affluent,** tributary, rich; **influence,** power or authority; **superfluous,** unnecessary, overflowing; **influx,** a flowing-in; **flux, confluence.**

**fortis** = strong, brave: **fort; forte,** that in which one excels; **fortify,** to make strong; **comfort,** ease, relief; **reinforce,**

to strengthen with men, or with material; **enforce,** compel, put in force.

**frater** = a brother: **fraternal,** brotherly; **fraternity,** brotherhood.

**fugio** (*fugitus*) = I flee: **fugitive,** one who flees; **centrifugal,** flying from a centre; **refuge,** a place of safety.

**gero** (*gestus*) = I bear, carry: **gesture,** a movement of the body; **jest,** a joke; **belligerent,** a person or party waging war.

**gradior** (*gressus*) = I step: **grade,** a step in rank; **degrade,** to lower; **retrograde,** going backward; **gradual,** by degrees.

**homo** = a man: **human,** pertaining to mankind; **homicide,** manslaughter; **humane,** kind, merciful.

**impero** = I command: **imperative,** that which must be done; **emperor,** a ruler; **empire,** region ruled over; **imperious,** commanding, haughty.

**insula** = an island: **insular,** belonging to an island; **insulate,** to separate from; **peninsula,** almost an island; **peninsular,** relating to a peninsula.

**iudex** (*judicis*) = a judge: **judge; judgement,** act of judging; **judicious,** wise or discreet; **prejudice,** unreasonable illwill or favour towards; **misjudge,** to judge wrongly.

**jungo** (*junctus*) = I join: **join; joint; junction,** a joining; **juncture,** a place of joining, a point of time; **adjoining,** lying near.

**lego** (*lectus*) = I select, I read: **legend,** a story handed down; **legible,** able to be read; **lecture,** an address; **eligible,** worthy to be chosen; **dialect,** branch of a language; **élite,** the chosen; **select,** to choose; **elegant,** neat, choice; **legion, elector, college.**

**lex** (*legis*) = a law: **legal,** pertaining to law; **legislate,** to make laws; **legitimate,** according to law; **privilege,** a special right.

**locus** = a place: **local,** belonging to a place; **locality,** district; **dislocate,** to put out of joint; **locate,** to fix the position of.

**loquor** (*locutus*) = I speak: **loquacity,** talkativeness; **eloquence,** fluent speech; **elocution,** art of correct speaking; **soliloquy,** speech to oneself; **ventriloquist.**

**magnus** = great: **magnitude,** size; **magnify,** to make large; **main.**

**male** = bad, ill: **malcontent,** a discontented person; **malefactor,** an ill-doer; **malady,** illness; **malice,** ill-feeling.

**mare** = the sea: **marine,** belonging to the sea; **mariner,** a sailor; **maritime,** pertaining to the sea; **submarine.**

**Mars** = God of War: **martial,** war-like.

**mater** = a mother: **matron,** a married woman; **maternal,** motherly; **matrimony,** marriage.

**metior** (*mensus*) = I measure: **mensuration,** the measuring of lengths, areas, etc.; **immense.**

**migro** = I migrate: **migration,** act of travelling; **immigrant,** one coming in; **emigrant,** one leaving; **transmigrate,** to pass to one country through another; **migratory,** moving to another country as the seasons change.

**miles** (*militis*) = a soldier: **military,** pertaining to soldiers; **militia,** a body of soldiers; **militant,** fighting (adj.); **militate.**

**mitto** (*missus*) = I send: **missile,** something thrown; **mission,** a sending; **missionary, admit, commit, dismiss, emit, omit.**

**mors** (*mortis*) = death: **mortal,** deadly; **immortal,** undying; **mortgage,** a pledge; **post-mortem, mortify.**

**multus** = many: **multitude,** a crowd; **multiply,** to increase.

**nauta** = a sailor: **nautical,** relating to sailors or navigation.

**navis** = a ship: **naval,** pertaining to ships; **navy,** a fleet of ships; **navigate,** to sail; **circumnavigate,** to sail round; **navigator,** a sailor, one who directs the course of a ship.

**nox** (*noctis*) = night: **nocturnal,** by night; **equinox,** equal day and night; **equinoctial,** relating to the equinoxes.

**omnis** = all: **omnibus,** a coach; **omnivorous,** devouring all things.

**opus** (*operis*) = work: **operate,** to work; **operation; manoeuvre,** a skilful plan or movement; **opera,** a musical drama.

**pater** = a father: **paternal,** like a father; **patriarch,** head of family; **patron,** a protector; **pattern, patrimony.**

**patior** (*passus*) = I suffer: **patience,** ability to endure; **passion,** strong feeling; **passive,** suffering, offering no opposition; **compassion,** suffering with, pity.

**patria** = fatherland: **patriot,** a lover of his country; **expatriate,** to banish; **compatriot,** a fellow-countryman.

**pax** (*pacis*) = peace: **pacify,** to quieten; **pacific,** peaceful.

**pes** (*pedis*) = a foot: **pedal,** part of an instrument or machine worked by the foot; **impede,** to hinder; **pedestrian,** a walker; **biped,** an animal with two feet; **quadruped,** a four-footed animal; **expedite,** to hasten; **pedestal, centipede.**

**pono** (*positus*) = I place: **position,** where placed; **compound,** a mixture; **deposit,** to put down; **impose,** to put upon.

**porto** = I bear, carry: **porter, portable,** able to be carried; **portmanteau,** a travelling-trunk; **import, export, transport.**

**primus** = first: **prime,** excellent, best; **primitive,** uncivilized, simple, as in early times; **primrose; premier,** chief minister; **prince; primeval,** ancient; **primary, primer.**

**quaero** (*quaesitus*) = I seek; **query,** an inquiry; **quest,** a search; **acquire,** to obtain; **requisite,** something needed.

**sanguis** = blood: **sanguine,** hopeful; **sanguinary,** blood-thirsty.

**satis** = enough: **satisfy,** to give enough; **satiate,** give or to have more than enough.

**sentio** (*sensus*) = I feel, think: **sensation,** feeling; **sensible,** having sense; **sentence,** judge's decision; **assent, dissent.**

**specio** = I see, look: **species,** kind or sort; **specimen,** a sample; **spectacle,** a sight; **prospect,** outlook, view; **aspect,** appearance.

**spiro** = I breathe: **inspire,** breathe into, inhale; **expire,** breathe out, die; **expiration,** act of breathing out, dying, coming to an end; **expiry, sprite, conspirator.**

**sto** (*status*) = I stand: **stable,** steady; **status,** rank or standing.

**tango** (*tactus*) = I touch: **contact,** touch; **contagion,** spread of disease by contact; **tact,** skill in managing people; **contiguous,** adjoining; **contingent, tangent.**

**teneo** (*tentus*) = I hold: **tenable,** capable of being held or defended; **tenant,** one who holds property by paying rent; **lieutenant,** a military officer.

**terra** = the earth: **terrace,** a bank of earth; **territory,** country.

**traho** (*tractus*) = I draw: **trace,** to draw over; **track,** path marked or beaten out; **contract,** an agreement; **retreat,** to retire.

**valeo** = I am well, strong: **valediction,** a farewell; **valiant,** brave; **convalescence,** state of recovering health; **prevail,** to overcome; **avail.**

**veho** (*vectus*) = I carry: **vehicle,** a carriage; **convey,** transport.

**venio** (*ventus*) = I come: **venture,** a risky undertaking; **avenue,** an approach; **revenue, advent.**

**verto** = I turn: **vertical,** upright; **convert,** to turn to, change.

**volo** = I wish: **volunteer,** one who offers his services; **benevolent.**

**voro** = I devour: **voracious,** greedy; **carnivorous,** flesh-eating; **insectivorous, omnivorous.**

**voco** = I call; **vocal; revoke,** to call back; **vocative.**

## GREEK ROOTS

**arche** = government: **anarchy,** want of government, law, or order; **anarchist,** a promoter of anarchy.

**aristos** = best, noblest: **aristocracy,** the nobility.

**astron** = a star: **astronomy,** study or science of the stars.

**atmos** = vapour: **atmosphere,** gases surrounding the earth.

**bapto** = I dip in water: **baptize,** to christen.

**baros** = weight: **barometer,** instrument for measuring the weight of the air; **barometric, barograph, isobar.**

**bios** = life: **biology,** science of animal life; **biological.**

**christos** = anointed: **Christian,** follower of Christ (the Anointed); **Christianity.**

**chronos** = time: **chronic,** lasting a long time; **chronicle,** a continuous record of events in order of time; **chronometer,** instrument for measuring time, accurately adjusted watch.

**crypto** = I hide: **crypt,** underground cell or chapel; **cryptic,** hidden, secret.

**cyclos** = a circle: **cycle,** circle or round of years, regular recurrence of events; **bicycle, tricycle, cyclist.**

**deka** = ten: **decade,** period of ten years; **decagon,** a ten-sided figure.

**demos** = the people: **democracy,** government by the people; **democrat,** supporter of government by the people.

**despotes** = a tyrant: **despot,** ruler with absolute power, tyrant; **despotic,** having absolute power, tyrannical.

**gamos** = marriage: **bigamy,** having two wives or two husbands at once; **monogamy,** marriage to one wife or husband only.

**ge** = the earth: **geology,** study of the earth's crust; **geography,** study of man in relation in his earthly environment; **geometry,** lit. earth measurement, now a branch of mathematics.

**genos** = kind or race: **genealogy,** history of descent of families, pedigree.

**gramma** = a letter: **grammar,** study of right use of language; **telegram, marconigram; gramophone,** instrument for recording and reproducing sounds; **programme.**

**grapho** = I write: **graph,** representation by means of lines; **graphic,** vividly described; **autograph,** signature; **graphite,** blacklead; **telegraph, paragraph.**

**helios** = the sun: **heliograph,** instrument for signalling by reflectors.

**horama** = a view: **panorama,** a view in all directions.

**hydor** = water: **hydrogen,** gas which in combination with oxygen produces water; **hydrant,** appliance by which water is drawn from a main pipe; **hydraulic,** operated by water power; **hydrostatic.**

**isos** = equal: **isosceles,** having two equal sides (used of triangle); **isotherm,** imaginary line connecting places having same mean temperature; **isobar.**

**logos** = a word: **dialogue,** conversation; **prologue,** preface, introductory verses before a play; **epilogue,** conclusion of book or play.

**mania** = madness: **mania,** insanity; **maniac,** madman.

**metron** = a measure: **barometer; thermometer,** instrument for measuring temperature; **chronometer.**

**micros** = small: **microscope,** instrument for magnifying small objects; **microphone,** instrument for rendering faintest sounds audible.

**monos,** alone: **monopoly,** sole right to own or sell anything; **monopolize,** to obtain a monopoly of anything; **monologue,** speech uttered by one person; **monogram,** several letters (e.g., one's initials) interwoven to make one figure; **monomania,** madness on one subject; **monoplane, monotype, monocle.**

**pan, pantos** = all: **panorama; panacea,** a cure-all; **pan-Anglican,** for all Christians of the Anglican Church; **pan-German.**

**pathos** = feeling: **pathetic,** causing pity, touching; **sympathy,** feeling with, compassion; **apathy, antipathy.**

**philos** = loving: **philosopher,** lover of wisdom; **philosophy.**

**phone** = sound: **phonic,** relating to sound; **telephone,** instrument for transmitting speech to a distance; **phonograph,** Edison's instrument for recording and reproducing sounds; **gramophone, phonetics, radiophone.**

**phos, photos** = light: **photograph,** picture produced by the action of light; **photography, phosphorus.**

**polis** = a city: **metropolis,** mother-city, capital.

**poly** = many: **Polynesia,** many islands; **polysyllable.**

**scopeo** = I see: **telescope,** instrument for examining objects at a distance; **microscope, periscope.**

**sophos** = wise: **philosopher, sophist.**

**tele** = at a distance: **telescope, telegraph, telephone, television, teleprinter, telepathy.**

**thermos** = heat: **thermos, thermometer.**

**tonos** = a tone or sound: **monotone,** a single unvarying sound; **monotony,** dull uniformity of sound; **monotonous,** unpleasant sameness of tone; **tonic.**

**tyrannos** = a ruler: **tyrant,** formerly any absolute ruler, now used only in a bad sense; **tyrannous, tyrannical.**

## WORDS OF FRENCH ORIGIN

**aide-de-camp** (aid′ de-kanh′): a general's or governor's staff officer.

**amateur** (am′-a-ture or am′-a-ter): a novice or beginner, not a professional.

**apropos** (ap-ro-po′): to the purpose, appropriately.

**avoirdupois** (av′-er-du-poiz′): referring to weight, the measure of weight.

**bayonet** (bay′-on-et): a short pointed steel weapon attachable to a rifle.

**blancmange** (bla-manzh′): a sweet made from cornflour boiled in milk and eaten when cold and set.

**bouquet** (boo-kay′): a bunch of flowers.

**brunette** (broo-net′): a dark-complexioned young woman, opposite of *blonde.*

**brusque** (broosk): blunt, gruff.

**bureau** (biu′-roh): office.

**camouflage** (kam′-oo-flahzh): concealment.

**chamois** (sham'-wah): a breed of goat, native of Swiss mountains.

**château** (shat'-o'): a castle.

**chauffeur** (sho-fur'): professional driver of a car.

**chef** (shef): a master-cook.

**chevalier** (shev-al'-i-ay): a knight.

**chic** (sheek): smart, stylish.

**connoisseur** (kon'-e-sur'): an expert judge of anything costly, such as wines, cigars, jewellery, pictures.

**coupé** (koo-pay): a two-seater motor car.

**coquette** (ko-ket'): a flirt.

**croquet** (kro'-kay): a lawn game.

**crochet** (kro'-shay): a kind of fancy work, made with a hook, in cotton, silk or wool.

**cuisine** (kwee-zeen'): the kitchen, the style or quality of cooking.

**cul-de-sac** (kool'-de-sak'): a blind alley.

**debris** (deb'-ree): a heap of ruins, accumulated fragments.

**début** (day'-boo): a first appearance on the stage or in society.

**dénouement** (day-noo'-manh): the outcome, the end or climax of an incident or story.

**depot** (dep'-o): a store for goods.

**eau-de-cologne** (o'-de ko-lone): a perfume, or toilet water.

**éclat** (ay-klah'): splendour, show, display.

**élite** (ay-leet'): the select, the pick of society, persons of superior rank or intellect.

**ennui** (onh-wee'): weariness, tedium.

**equerry** (ek'-wer-i): a master of the horse, a mounted military servant.

**esprit de corps** (ess-pree'-de-kor): comradeship.

**etiquette** (et-i-ket'): the usages of polite society, good manners.

**fête** (fayt): feast, festival, holiday.

**fracas** (fra-kah'): a dispute or fight.

**fragile** (fraj'-ile): delicate, frail, slight, easily broken.

**garage** (ga'-rahzh): a motor-car shed.

**hangar** (hang'-ar): a shelter or shed for aeroplanes.

**haricot** (har'-i-ko): a French bean.

**harlequin** (har'-le-kwin): a clown in a pantomime.

**lieu** (loo): place, stead, as *in lieu of*.

**limousine** (lim-oo-zeen'): a large saloon motor car.

**manoeuvre** (man-oo'-ver): a skilful or shrewd course of action.

**marquee** (mar-kee'): a large field-tent.

**massage** (mas-sahzh'): the rubbing or kneading of the body to cure ailments.

**matinée** (mat-i-nay'): an afternoon entertainment.

**mirage** (mi-rahzh'): an optical illusion taking the form of a false appearance of water.

**omelet** (om'-e-let or om'-let): a dish made of eggs and milk beaten together and fried.

**patois** (pat'-wah): a local or provincial dialect, corrupt speech.

**piquant** (pee'-kant): sharp to the taste; lively and interesting.

**pique** (peek): slight resentment, irritation or vexation.

**prestige** (pres-teezh'): authority based on fame or reputation.

**protégé** (prot'-ay-zhay): a person under one's protection, a ward.

**queue** (kew): tail, plait, line of waiting persons.

**reconnoitre** (rek-o-noy'-ter): to spy out for a military purpose, give a preliminary survey.

**régime** (ray-zheem'): a system of conducting affairs, method of rule.

**rendezvous** (ranh'-day'-voo'): a place of meeting, an appointment, tryst.

**reservoir** (rez'-er-vwahr): a storage place for water or gas.

**restaurant** (res'-to-rahn'): a dining saloon or eating-house.

**reveille** (re-vel'-i): morning drum or bugle to awaken soldiers.

**role** (role): part played by an actor.

**sabot** (sa'-bo): a wooden shoe.

**souvenir** (su'-ve-neer'): a token of remembrance.

**suède** (swayd): tanned kid-skin.

**trait** (tray): a particular feature or characteristic, mental or physical.

**valet** (val'-ay): a gentleman's personal servant.

# WORDS DERIVED FROM PROPER NOUNS

*From names of persons:*

**August,** the eighth month (Augustus, Roman emperor).

**blucher,** a strong leather half-boot (Marshall Blücher).

**bohemian,** a person who disregards social conventions (Bohemia).

**boycott,** to have no dealings with (Captain Boycott, an Irishman, so treated in 1880).

**brougham,** a one-horse closed carriage (Lord Brougham, a British statesman).

**dahlia,** a large-flowered garden-plant (Dahl, a Swedish botanist).

**Friday,** the sixth day of the week (Freya, pagan goddess).

**galvanic,** pertaining to galvanism, a form of electricity (Galvani, the discoverer).

**gipsy,** member of a wandering race, the Romanies (Egyptian).

**gladstone,** a kind of light travelling-bag (W. E. Gladstone, British statesman).

**guillotine,** a machine for beheading people (Dr Guillotin, the inventor).

**Jesuit,** a member of a religious order (the Society of Jesus).

**July,** the seventh month (Julius Caesar, the Roman emperor).

**macadamize,** to cover a road with broken stones, so as to give it a smooth hard surface (McAdam, the inventor of metalled roads).

**Mahometan,** a follower of Mahomet (Mahomet, the great prophet of Arabia).

**marconigram,** a wireless telegram (Marconi, the inventor of wireless telegraphy).

**martial**, warlike (Mars, the Roman god of war).

**May,** the fifth month (Maius, the month sacred to Maia, the mother of Mercury).

**mercurial,** active, changeable (Mercury, the messenger of the gods).

**panic,** extreme fright (Pan, god of the woods, who excited terror by various means).

**tantalize,** to torment by offering and then withdrawing someing greatly desired (Tantalus, in Greek mythology, was condemned to stand up to his chin in water beneath branches laden with fruit, each receding from him as he tried to drink or eat).

**tawdry,** showy without taste, gaudy (St Awdrey = St Ethelreda, who had once been a lover of finery).

**Thursday,** the fifth day of the week (Thor, the pagan god of thunder).

**vandalism,** hostility to arts or literature (Vandals, a fierce North German race of barbarians who overran Europe in the middle ages).

**wellingtons,** long riding boots (Duke of Wellington).

### From names of places:

**artesian,** a perpendicular boring into the earth, through which water rises (Artois, in the north of France).

**bayonet,** a short steel stabbing weapon fixed to a rifle-muzzle (Bayonne, a town in the south-west of France).

**calico,** a kind of cotton cloth (Calicut, a town in the south-west of India).

**cambric,** a kind of fine white linen (Cambrai, a town in France).

**canter,** an easy gallop (Canterbury, a cathedral city in England to which pilgrimages were made).

**champagne,** a light sparkling wine (Champagne, a district in the south-west of France).

**cherry,** a small luscious stone-fruit (Cerasus, a seaport in Asia Minor).

**chocolate,** a food prepared by griding cacao berries (Choco, in Mexico).

**cognac** (pron. kon'-yak), a superior quality of brandy (Cognac, in France).

**damask,** figured material of linen, cotton or silk (Damascus, in Syria).

**ermine,** animal yielding a valuable white fur (Armenia, a country to the south-east of the Black Sea).

**gin,** a kind of spirit distilled from grain (Geneva, a town in Western Switzerland).

**guinea,** an English gold coin, no longer in use; 21s. (Guinea, in Western Africa).

**indigo,** a blue dye (India, whence the dye first came).

**Jew,** a Hebrew or Israelite (Judah, a district in Palestine).

**limerick,** a form of nonsense verse in five lines (Limerick, in Ireland).

**madeira,** a rich wine (Madeira Islands, north-west of Africa).

**magnet,** a piece of iron that attracts iron or steel (Magnesia, Thessaly).

**meander,** to take a winding course (Maiandros, a winding river in Asia Minor).

**milliner,** a maker of ladies' hats (Milan, in Italy).

**morocco,** a fine leather made of goat-skin (Morocco, in north-west Africa).

**muslin,** a fine soft cotton fabric (Mosul, in Mesopotamia).

**nankeen,** a yellowish cotton cloth (Nanking, in China).

**port,** a dark-red wine (Oporto, a town in Portugal).

**sherry,** a white wine (Xeres, a town near Cadiz in Spain).

**spaniel,** a kind of dog (Spain).

**topaz,** a kind of gem (Topazos, an island in the Red Sea).

**worsted,** twisted thread or yarn spun out of long combed wool (Worstead, a village in England near Norwich).

**pistol,** a small hand-gun (Pistoja or Pistola, a town in Italy).

# 4. WORDS TO BE DISTINGUISHED

**absolute,** complete, unlimited.
**obsolete,** out-of-date, antiquated.

**alley,** a narrow lane.
**ally,** a helper, confederate.

**analogy,** likeness, resemblance.
**allegory,** a description of one thing under the image of another, as in Bunyan's *Pilgrim's Progress*.

**annoy,** to anger, to irritate.
**aggravate,** to make worse.

**ballad,** a song or poem.
**ballet,** a dance.
**ballot,** secret voting.

**cartridge,** a case containing the charge for a gun.
**cartilage,** an elastic, gristly substance in the joints of bones.

**cemetery,** a human burial place.
**seminary,** a religious college.

**censer,** pan for burning incense.
**censor,** a critic, judge.

**civility,** politeness, good breeding.
**servility,** slavish obedience.

**contemptuous,** showing contempt.
**contemptible,** worthy of contempt.

**diffuse** (s = z), to spread.
**diffuse** (s = ss), wordy.

**economic,** relating to wealth or material welfare.
**economical,** showing economy, frugal.

**elicit,** to draw out of, educe.
**illicit,** illegal, unlicensed.

**elusion,** an escape by stratagem, evasion.
**illusion,** a deceptive appearance.
**delusion,** a false idea or belief.

**eminent,** famous, distinguished.
**imminent,** near-at-hand, threatening.

**explicit,** clearly stated, plain.
**implicit,** implied, unquestioning.

**expedient,** advisable, suitable.
**expedite,** to remove obstacles from, hasten the progress of.

**gauze,** a fine thin fabric of silk or wire.

**gauge,** a measuring rod or standard of measure.

**gouge,** a chisel with a hollow blade for cutting grooves or holes.

**gorilla,** a huge African ape.

**guerilla,** a fighter in a small independent force engaged in warfare.

**incredible,** unbelievable (of a statement).

**incredulous,** hard to convince (of a person).

**ingenious,** clever, skilful.

**ingenuous,** frank, open.

**inveterate,** firmly established, deeply rooted.

**invertebrate,** without vertebral column or backbone.

**irreverent,** not reverent, showing no respect for sacred things.

**irrelevant,** not relating to, not connected with.

**loath,** unwilling, disliking.

**loathe,** to dislike greatly, detest.

**obverse,** turned towards, side of a coin containing the head.

**reverse,** opposite, the back of a coin.

**paradox,** that which is apparently absurd but really true.

**parody,** an imitation of a poem so as to produce a ridiculous effect.

**phase,** aspect or appearance at a given time.

**phrase,** a distinct group of words forming part of a sentence.

**practical,** useful.

**practicable,** able to be put into practice.

**prescribe,** to give directions for, as a remedy.

**proscribe,** to put beyond the protection of the law; to forbid.

**prophecy** (n.), a foretelling.

**prophesy** (v.), to foretell the future.

**prosecute,** to bring to trial.

**persecute,** to annoy, harass.

**respectfully,** showing respect.

**respectively,** each in turn.

**reverent,** devout, religious.

**relevant,** relating to.

**statue,** a metal or stone figure.

**statute,** a law.

**summon,** to call with authority.

**summons,** act of calling, a legal document demanding attendance at court.

**veracious,** truthful.

**voracious,** ravenously greedy.

## 5. WORDS OFTEN MISPRONOUNCED

**advertisement** (ad-ver'tiz-ment): making known, as by public notice in a newspaper.

**aerial** (ayr-i-al): belonging to the air; the aerial wire of a radio or television installation.

**aerodrome** (ayr'-o-drome): a depot for aeroplanes.

**analogous** (a-nal'-o-gus): similar to, resembling.

**anemone** (a-nem'-o-ne): a plant of the crowfoot family.

**armistice** (ar'-miss-tiss): a brief cessation of warfare, a truce.

**asparagus** (ass-par'-a-gus): a tall-growing, bushy plant whose young shoots are eaten as a vegetable.

**athenaeum** (ath-en-ee'-um): a public institution for lectures or reading.

**awry** (a-ri'): twisted to one side, distorted.

**Beauchamp** (beech'-am): a surname.

**centenary** (sen-teen'-a-ry): a hundred years.

**chagrin** (sha-green'): vexation, annoyance.

**chastisement** (chass'-tiz-ment): punishment.

**chattel** (chat'-el): a piece of personal property.

**Cholmondeley** (chum'-ley): a surname.

**complaisance** (kom-play'-zanse): desire to please.

**complaisant** (kom-play-'zant): obliging.

**compromise** (kom'-pro-mize): mutual concession.

**comptroller** (kon-tro-ler): one who checks accounts, an auditor.

**conjure** (kun'-jer): to implore; to juggle.

**controversy** (kon'-tro-ver-sy): argument, dispute.

**contumely** (kon'-tu-me-ly): rudeness, insolence.

**conversant** (kon-ver'-sant): well-informed.

**covetous** (kuv'-e-tus): inordinately greedy of possession.

**dahlia** (day'-lee-a): a plant of the aster family.

**desultory** (dess'-ul-to-ry): rambling, inconstant.

**dishevelled** (di-shev'-elled): with the hair in disorder.

**embryo** (em'-bri-o): a seed or young animal in first stages of
 growth.

**extant** (eks'-tant): still existing.

**extempore** (eks-tem'-po-ri): without preparation.

**gesture** (jes'-ture): a motion of the body or limbs.

**geyser** (gay'-zer): a spouting fountain of boiling water.

**government** (gov'-ern-ment): the system of rule in a country,
 the rulers themselves.

**heinous** (hay'nus): extremely wicked.

**hygiene** (hy'-jeen): the science of health.

**hysterics** (hiss-ter'-iks): a condition of violent emotion.

**impromptu** (im-promp'-tu): prompt, ready, on the spur of
 the moment.

**improvize** (im'-pro-vize): to devise on the spur of the moment.

**indictment** (in-dite'-ment): a formal accusation.

**interesting** (in'-ter-est-ing): engaging the attention, entertain-
 ing.

**inveigh** (in-vay'): to speak violently (against).

**irrelevant** (i-rel'-i-vant): not relating to, that does not apply.

**khedive** (ke-deev'): title of former rulers of Egypt.

**laboratory** (lab'-o-ra-to-ry): a room in which scientific
 experiments are made.

**lackadaisical** (lak-a-day'-zi-kal): affectedly sentimental.

**longitude** (lon'-ji-tude): distance of a place east or west of the
 Greenwich meridian.

**miscellany** (miss-el'-a-ny): a collection of writings on different
 topics.

**obstreperous** (ob-strep'-er-us): loud, noisy, clamorous.

**pantomime** (pan'-to-mime): a showy play telling some well-known story, with music and dancing.

**paralyse** (par'-a-lize): to strike with paralysis.

**paralysis** (par-al'-i-siss): loss of muscular power or other bodily power, palsy.

**paralytic** (par-a-lyt'-ik): afflicted with paralysis.

**pariah** (pa'-ri-a): an outcast from society.

**piano** (pi-an'o or pi-ah'-no): a musical instrument.

**posthumous** (pos'-tu-mus): born after the father's death.

**ransacked** (ran'-sakt): thoroughly searched, plundered.

**relevant** (rel'-i-vant): bearing upon, related to.

**respite** (res'-pit): temporary suspension of anything, such as labour, punishment, etc.

**rout** (rowt): utter defeat and disorder.

**route** (root): course taken.

**schedule** (shed'-ule): a written statement or list.

**sesame** (sess'-a-me): an East-Indian herb; a password.

**simile** (sim'-i-lee): a figure of speech based on comparison.

**sojourn** (so'-jurn): stay in a place for a time.

**suave** (swahve): pleasingly smooth in manner.

**variegated** (va'-ri-e-gat-ed): marked with different colours.

**venison** (ven'-i-zun or ven'-zun): the flesh of deer.

**Warwick** (war'-ik): an English place-name and surname.

# 6. ANTONYMS

| Nouns | | Adjectives | |
|---|---|---|---|
| poi'son | an'tidote | op'tional / vol'untary | compul'sory |
| goodwill | malice | | |
| in'gress | e'gress | benev'olent | malev'olent |
| civilization | sav'agery | per'manent | tem'porary |
| max'imum | min'imum | obverse' | reverse' |
| le'niency | sever'ity | prov'ident | improv'ident |

|  | Nouns |  | Adjectives |
| --- | --- | --- | --- |
| aristoc'racy | democ'racy | aristocrat'ic | plebe'ian |
| lat'itude | lon'gitude | orient'al | occident'al |
| antece'dent | con'sequent | affirm'ative | neg'ative |
| com'edy | trag'edy | pos'itive | |
| convic'tion | acquit'tal | indig'enous | exot'ic |
| tranquill'ity | disqui'et | terres'trial | celes'tial |
| plaint'iff | defend'ant | or'thodox | het'erodox |
| man'uscript | print | co-or'dinate | subor'dinate |
| op'timist | pes'simist | gen'uine | count'erfeit |
| op'timism | pes'simism | prolif'ic | ster'ile |

|  | Verbs |  |  |
| --- | --- | --- | --- |
| convict' | acquit' | plant | erad'icate |
| retard' | accel'erate | impede' | ex'pedite |
| improve' | deter'iorate | alle'viate | ag'gravate |
| eu'logize | dispar'age | embell'ish | disfig'ure |
|  |  | beau'tify | |

## 7. WORD-BUILDING GROUPS

| rhyme | reveal' | exclude' | exhaust' |
| --- | --- | --- | --- |
| rhythm | revealed' | exclu'sion | exhaus'tion |
| rhyth'mical | revela'tion | exclu'sive | inexhaust'ible |
| em'phasis | cov'et | ini'tial | accom'pany |
| em'phasise | cov'eting | ini'tiate | accom'paniment |
| emphat'ic | cov'eted | initia'tion | accom'panied |
| emphat'ically | cov'etous | ini'tiative | accom'panist |
| unemphat'ic | cov'etousness | ini'tiatory | accom'panying |
| envi'rons | ig'nominy | discourse' | pecu'niary |
| envi'ronment | ignomin'ious | discur'sive | impecu'nious |

| | | | |
|---|---|---|---|
| proceed′ | precede′ | fed′erate | elec′tric |
| proceed′ing | preced′ing | federa′tion | electric′ity |
| proceed′ed | preced′ed | fed′eral | electri′cian |
| proced′ure | prec′edent | confed′erate | elec′trify |
| process′ion | prec′edented | confed′eracy | elec′trocute |
| | | | |
| sys′tem | cen′tury | acquire | in′sulate |
| sys′temat′ic | cen′tenary | acquisi′tion | in′sulator |
| sys′tematize | centen′nial | acquis′itive | insula′tion |
| | | | |
| tradi′tion | cir′cuit | di′agnose | ec′stasy |
| tradi′tional | circu′itous | diagno′sis | ecstat′ic |
| | | | |
| archa′ic | colos′sus | im′becile | ef′ficacy |
| ar′chaism | colos′sal | imbecil′ity | effica′cious |
| | | | |
| af′fable | preside′ | ed′ucate | or′ganize |
| af′fably | pres′ident | educa′tion | organi′zer |
| affabil′ity | presiden′tial | educa′tional | organiza′tion |
| affableness | pres′idency | ed′ucative | disor′ganize |
| | | | |
| antique′ | retain′ | mature′ | repute′ |
| anti′quity | retain′er | matured′ | reputa′tion |
| an′tiquated | reten′tion | matur′ity | rep′utable |
| antiquar′ian | reten′tive | immature′ | disrep′utable |
| | | | |
| fanat′ic | ver′tebra | phrase | mort′gage |
| fanat′ical | ver′tebral | par′aphrase | mort′gager |
| fanat′icism | inver′tebrate | periph′rasis | mort′gagee |
| | | | |
| dictate′ | cru′cify | rotate′ | mor′tal |
| dicta′tion | cru′cifix | rota′tion | immor′tal |
| dic′tatory | crucifix′ion | ro′tatory | immor′talize |
| dictator′ial | cru′ciform | ro′tary | mortal′ity |
| | | | |
| tem′porary | emul′sion | fulfil′ | syn′onym |
| contem′porary | emul′sify | fulfil′ment | synon′ymous |
| | | | |
| annex′ | o′men | artic′ulate | antith′esis |
| annexa′tion | om′inous | inartic′ulate | antithet′ical |

au'gur        stim'ulus        cap'able        capa'cious
au'gury       stim'ulate       incap'able      capac'ity
inau'gurate   stim'ulant       incapabil'ity   incapac'ity

gal'vanize    concil'iate      ar'biter        har'mony
gal'vanism    concilia'tion    ar'bitrate      harmo'nious
galvan'ic     concil'iatory    arbitra'tion    har'monize

simulta'neous      util'ity    sub'stitute     indepen'dent
contempora'neous  u'tilize     substitu'tion   indepen'dence

so'cial       phys'ic          lo'cal          gov'ern
so'cialism    phys'ical        locate'         gov'ernor
socialis'tic  phys'ically      locat'ing       gov'ernment
so'cially     physique'        loca'tion       ungov'ernable
associa'tion  physi'cian       local'ity       gov'erness
asso'ciated   physiol'ogy      lo'calized      misgov'ern

con'tact      vi'tal           fas'cinate      ir'ritate
conta'gious   vital'ity        fascina'tion    irrita'tion
contig'uous   vi'talize        fas'cinating    ir'ritable

nor'mal       char'acter       tes'timony      allege'
normal'ity    char'acterize    testimo'nial    alleg'ing
abnor'mal     characteri'zation tes'tament     alleged'
abnorm'ity    characteris'tic  attest'         allega'tion

respon'sible  apply'           es'timate       op'portune
responsibil'ity applica'tion   es'timable      opportu'nity
irrespon'sible ap'plicable     estima'tion     inop'portune

mili'tia      commend'         unite'          effec'tive
mil'itant     commenda'tion    u'nity          effec'tively
mil'itary     commend'able     u'nion          ineffec'tive
mil'itate     recommend'       u'nison         effec'tually
mil'itarism   recommenda'tion  u'nify          ineffec'tual

assem'ble     exam'ple         fi'nite         mag'net
assem'bly     exem'plify       def'inite       mag'netism
assem'blage   exem'plifies     in'finite       magnet'ic
dissem'ble    exem'plary       infin'ity       magne'to

| | | | |
|---|---|---|---|
| inadver'tent | guarantee' | vo'cal | rem'edy |
| inadver'tently | guaranteed' | voca'tion | reme'diable |
| inadver'tence | guarantor' | voc'ative | reme'dial |
| | | | |
| mayor' | inher'it | anom'aly | cu'mulus |
| ma'yoral | inher'ited | anom'alies | cu'mulative |
| ma'yoralty | her'itage | anom'alous | accu'mulate |
| | | | |
| pre'cipice | explain' | econ'omy | dom'inate |
| precip'itous | explana'tion | econom'ic | predom'inate |
| precip'itate | explan'atory | econom'ical | dom'inant |
| precip'itated | inex'plicable | econ'omize | predom'inant |
| | | | |
| ef'ficacy | peruse' | po'tent | immune' |
| effica'cious | peru'sal | poten'tial | immu'nity |
| | | | |
| sum'mary | par'ish | represent' | con'trovert |
| sum'marize | paro'chial | represen'tative | |
| | | | con'troversy |
| | | | |
| type | sphere | al'ternate* | solic'it |
| typ'ical | spheric'ity | alter'nately | solic'itor |
| typ'ify | spher'ical | alter'native | solic'itude |
| typog'raphy | hem'isphere | alterna'tion | solic'itous |
| | | | |
| ge'nial | disci'ple | tran'quil | hu'mour |
| conge'nial | dis'cipline | tranquill'ity | hu'morous |
| | | | |
| in'teger | dra'ma | au'dible | prohib'it |
| in'tegral | dramat'ic | inau'dible | prohibi'tion |
| integ'rity | dram'atize | au'dibly | prohib'itive |
| | | | |
| finance' | apol'ogy | hered'ity | reminis'cent |
| finan'cial | apol'ogize | hered'itary | reminis'cence |
| | | | |
| op'timist | pes'simist | resist' | men'tal |
| op'timism | pes'simism | resist'ible | men'tally |
| optimis'tic | pessimis'tic | irresist'ible | mental'ity |

*Or al-ter'-nate.

71

| hon'our | vacate' | or'igin | comprehend' |
|---------|---------|---------|-------------|
| hon'ourable | va'cant | orig'inal | comprehen'sion |
| dishon'our | vaca'tion | aborig'inal | comprehen'sive |
| dishon'ourable | vac'uum | aborig'ines | |
| hon'orary | evac'uate | orig'inate | comprehen'sible |
| | | | incomprehen'sible |

| com'fort | discom'fit | absorb' | lit'eral |
|----------|------------|---------|----------|
| com'forted | discom'fiting | absorb'ent | lit'erary |
| com'fortable | discom'fited | absorp'tion | illit'erate |
| discom'fort | discom'fiture | absorp'tive | lit'erature |